LIFELONG KINDERGARTEN

LIFELONG KINDERGARTEN

Cultivating Creativity through Projects, Passion, Peers, and Play

MITCHEL RESNICK
WITH A FOREWORD BY SIR KEN ROBINSON

The MIT Press
Cambridge, Massachusetts
London, England

This book was set in ScalaSansPro and Scala by Toppan Best-set Premedia Limited. Printed and bound in the United States of America.

Library of Congress Cataloging-in-Publication Data is available.

ISBN: 978-0-262-03729-7

10　9　8　7　6　5　4　3　2　1

Photo credits:
Chapter 1: MIT Media Lab
Chapter 2: MIT Media Lab
Chapter 3: Sci-Bono Clubhouse
Chapter 4: Kelly Lorenz Imagery
Chapter 5: Exploratorium
Chapter 6: Exploratorium

CONTENTS

Human creativity moves hand in hand with technology. Over the course of history our tools have evolved from flint knives to the Large Hadron Collider and beyond. Whether they are mechanical or digital, simple or complex, tools facilitate our creativity in two ways. Initially, they extend our bodies and enable us to do things that are otherwise difficult or impossible. With ploughs we can cultivate, with telescopes we can see, with engines we can travel, far beyond the limits of our unassisted bodies. But tools do more than extend our bodies: they expand our minds. Technology facilitates ideas that might otherwise be inconceivable.

The plough was designed to turn over soil: in due course it overturned whole ways of life and gave rise to entirely new ones. When Galileo looked through his telescope he did more than see the planets in close-up: he reconceived the earth's place in the cosmos and fueled a religious revolution. In the 18th century, mechanical engines drove people faster than they could run: they also jump-started the Industrial Revolution and generated a torrent of innovations that reshaped the whole of civilization.

Mitchel Resnick has spent his professional life exploring the synergies between creativity and technology, especially for children. In *Lifelong Kindergarten*, he dispels common myths about creativity (that it is confined to the arts, for example), and he provides compelling examples and case studies of creative thinking in action and of its surprising outcomes. He also delves into the fascinating dynamics of creative thinking, and what he calls the Creative Learning Spiral. Through his groundbreaking work at the MIT Media Lab, he has contributed enormously to our conceptual understanding of these dynamics and of their importance for education. As you'll find here, the value of his work is more than academic. He and his teams have developed programs, devices, and activities that have catalyzed the creative capacities of millions of young people around the world.

Parents and educators often worry about how much time young people spend with digital devices. As Resnick notes, it's not the time spent but what they're doing with them that matters most. Some commercial programs and devices are sophisticated consumer distractions: their designers may have put a lot of creative thought into producing them, but it takes little or no creative thought to use them. Digital technologies can also be designed to facilitate creative thinking. Resnick has long experience in working with such technologies, from his pioneering work with the Scratch programming software to his longstanding creative collaboration with the LEGO Group, which has resulted in products and activities and that are intended to cultivate creative thinking in young people, and they do.

Why does creativity matter anyway? Because being creative is part of what it means to be human. Creativity is developing original ideas that have value, and it has driven human achievement on every front since the dawn of history. The roots of human creativity lie in our unique powers of imagination, the ability to bring to mind things that are not present to our senses. Creativity is a step beyond imagination: it is putting your imagination to work. Creativity is a practical as well as a conceptual process: how and what we create has much to do with the tools and materials we have available, and what we make of and with them.

Designing tools—digital or otherwise—is a creative enterprise in itself and like most others it evolves in the doing. It is a prime example of the Creative Learning Spiral in action. A prototype tool might work well enough but in the course of being used it may be improved in ways that weren't obvious or possible to begin with. Successive versions may be turned to other uses entirely and have an impacts far beyond the original. Think of the early versions of the printing press, the motorcar, the Internet, or the smartphone.

Creativity is not only incremental: it is collaborative. However original, creative thinking almost always builds on other people's ideas. Apple launched the iPhone in 2007. When it opened the App Store in 2008, there were 800 apps. There are now over two million, most of them neither developed nor anticipated by Apple. Illuminating the dynamics of creative thinking, and their implications for education, is another signature theme of this book.

There is a larger theme here too. Every child is born with immense natural talents. How they develop has much to do with the environment in which they are raised and the opportunities they are given. Education should be among the best of those opportunities. Too often it isn't. In many countries, formal education is mired in a dreary culture of testing and competition. That culture is now seeping down to early childhood education and risks stifling the nascent creative energies of the very young. At the heart of this book is an urgent call for education to change course.

Friedrich Froebel conceived of early education as a kindergarten because he understood, as gardeners do of plants, that children flourish best in certain conditions. The role of educators is to create those conditions. Froebel was promoting these practices in the 19th century as the Industrial Revolution was gathering force, and with it forms of mass education that were industrial in character. He had a hard struggle, and those who promote such child-centered ideas still do. These ideas are no less important for that. On the contrary, as we move deeper into the complex challenges of the 21st century, they are becoming more important.

For most of human history, the tools of creative production were in relatively few hands. The digital revolution has put sophisticated tools within reach of almost everyone. But even the most accessible of them are worthless without the ideas and expertise of those who use them. That is why this book matters. It is a grounded and visionary call for education as a whole to cultivate the ancient, creative powers that lie within us through the new tools we now have to do that. As Resnick pithily says, kindergarten is now becoming like the rest of school. In this book, he argues the opposite, that the rest of school (indeed, the rest of life) should become more like kindergarten. I'm sure he's right.

Sir Ken Robinson
Los Angeles, June 2017

CREATIVE LEARNING

FROM A TO X

On August 23, 2013, I met with the president of Tsinghua University, the leading engineering university in China. Because I'm a professor at Massachusetts Institute of Technology (MIT) and Tsinghua is known as the *MIT of China*, it's not so surprising that the two of us would meet. Perhaps more surprising is where we were meeting: at the LEGO toy company in Denmark.

The president of Tsinghua, Chen Jining, had traveled to the LEGO Group in search of a new approach to education and learning. The Chinese government had selected Tsinghua to lead a nationwide initiative on comprehensive university reform. Chen recognized that the Chinese educational system faced a serious problem—not just at the university level, but throughout the whole system, starting with the youngest children. The Chinese education system, Chen said, wasn't preparing students to meet the needs of an evolving society.

The problem wasn't visible by looking at students' grades and exam scores. In fact, many Chinese students were performing well according to traditional measures. At Tsinghua itself, almost all students had received excellent grades from elementary school through high school, and many continued to get A grades at Tsinghua. Chen referred to them as *A students*.

But Chen knew that something else was needed. He felt that many of the A students, despite their high grades and test scores, didn't have the creative, innovative spirit needed to succeed in today's society. Chen argued that China needed a new breed of students, which he called *X students*. Chen explained that X students are willing to take risks and try new things. They're eager to define their own problems rather than simply solve the ones in the textbook. It's X students who come up with the most innovative ideas and creative new directions.

Chen said that his top priority at Tsinghua was to produce more X students for Chinese society. He wanted to transform his university so that it would attract, encourage, and support X students. Chen came to visit the LEGO Group because he saw the company as a possible ally in his mission. When he watched children playfully building with LEGO bricks, he sensed that they were developing as X-style thinkers. They were constantly exploring, experimenting, and testing the boundaries—and developing as creative thinkers. He wanted to find more ways to cultivate that style of thinking at Tsinghua.

Although Chen was talking about students and schools in China, the situation is similar around the world. Most schools in most countries place a higher priority on teaching students to follow instructions and rules (becoming A students) than on helping students develop their own ideas, goals, and strategies (becoming X students). The goals and approaches of educational systems around the world have remained largely unchanged over the past century—but a growing number of people, like Chen, are beginning to recognize the need for change.

Part of the motivation for change is economic. Today's workplace is undergoing a radical transformation. Many jobs are disappearing as computers and robots take over routine tasks (and even nonroutine tasks)—and almost all jobs are changing as people and workplaces must continually adapt to a constant flow of new technologies, new sources of information, and new communication channels. In her book *Now You See It*, Cathy Davidson estimates that roughly two-thirds of today's grade-school students will end up doing work that hasn't been invented yet. For people to flourish in this rapidly changing landscape, the ability to think and act creatively is more important than ever before.

Creative thinking is needed outside of the workplace, too. The pace of change continues to accelerate in all types of activities, in all aspects of our lives. Today's young people will be confronted with new and unexpected situations throughout their lives. They must learn to deal creatively with uncertainty and change—not only in their work lives, but also in their personal lives (how to develop and sustain friendships in an era of ever-changing social networks) and their civic lives (how to participate meaningfully in communities that have ever-shifting needs and boundaries).

How can we help young people develop as creative thinkers so that they're prepared for life in this ever-changing world? That's the central question of this book—and it's the question that has motivated my work (and my life) over the past three decades.

I'm fortunate to work at the MIT Media Lab, a research lab full of X students and X researchers—people who are constantly exploring new ideas and inventing new possibilities. That's a great environment for me, but I'm frustrated so few people have access to these types of opportunities and inspirations elsewhere. My goal is to bring the Media Lab spirit of creativity and innovation to children around the world so that they too can grow up as X thinkers.

To make that happen, my research group at the Media Lab is focused on developing new technologies and activities to engage children in creative learning experiences. We've collaborated with the LEGO Group for more than 30 years, helping to develop new generations of construction kits—and helping to spread the gospel of playful learning with new partners, like Tsinghua University. We've also developed the Scratch programming language and online community, enabling millions of young people around the world to create and share their own interactive stories, games, and animations. And we helped establish the Computer Clubhouse network of after-school learning centers, where youth from low-income communities learn to express themselves creatively with new technologies.

In this book, I'll draw on stories and lessons from these projects to explore both the *why* and the *how* of creative thinking—building the case for why creative thinking is so important in today's world, and sharing strategies for how to help young people develop as creative thinkers.

The book is intended for anyone who cares about kids, learning, and creativity, whether you're a parent deciding on toys and activities for your children, an educator searching for new ways to help your students learn, a school administrator implementing new educational initiatives, a designer creating new products or activities for children, or simply someone who is curious about kids, learning, and creativity.

I expect the book will be of special interest if you're intrigued (or concerned) by the role of new technologies in children's lives. Although I'm actively involved in developing new technologies for children, I'm skeptical and worried about the ways that many technologies are entering children's lives. Most children's apps and high-tech toys aren't designed to support or encourage creative thinking. This book presents an alternative vision. It highlights how new technologies, if properly designed and supported, can expand opportunities for all children from all backgrounds to experiment, explore, and express themselves—and, in the process, develop as creative thinkers.

In my work, my ultimate goal is a world full of creative people— X people—who are constantly developing new possibilities for themselves and their communities. I believe this book is timely: There's a greater need for creative thinking today than ever before, and new technologies are offering new ways to help young people develop as creative thinkers. But I also believe that the core message of the book is timeless. Creative thinking has always been, and will always be, a central part of what makes life worth living. Life as a creative thinker can bring not only economic rewards, but also joy, fulfillment, purpose, and meaning. Children deserve nothing less.

LIFELONG KINDERGARTEN

As the year 1999 rolled into 2000, I participated in a conference session where people debated the greatest inventions of the previous thousand years. Some people argued that the printing press was the most important invention; others argued for the steam engine, the light bulb, or the computer.

My nomination for the greatest invention of the previous thousand years? Kindergarten.

That choice might seem surprising. Most people do not think of kindergarten as an invention, let alone an important invention. But kindergarten is a relatively new idea (less than 200 years old), and it represents an important departure from previous approaches to schooling. When Friedrich Froebel opened the world's first kindergarten in Germany in 1837, it wasn't simply a school for younger children. It was based on a radically different approach to education, fundamentally different from schools that came before.

Although Froebel certainly didn't know it at the time, he was inventing an approach to education that is ideally suited to the needs of the 21st century—and not just for five-year-olds, but for learners of all ages. Indeed, as I've thought about ways to help people develop as creative thinkers, much of my inspiration has come from the ways children learn in kindergarten. I've used the phrase *Lifelong Kindergarten* not just as the title of this book, but also as the name of my research group at MIT. I'm convinced that kindergarten-style learning is exactly what's needed to help people of all ages develop the creative capacities needed to thrive in today's rapidly changing society.

Before Froebel invented the first kindergarten in 1837, most schools were based on what might be called a *broadcast approach* to education; that is, the teacher stood in front of the classroom and broadcast information. Students sat in their seats and carefully wrote down the information, word for word. From time to time, students would recite back what they had written down. Classroom discussion happened rarely, if at all.

Froebel knew that this approach wouldn't work for five-year-olds. He understood that young children learn best by interacting with the world around them. So, in setting up the first kindergarten, Froebel shifted from a broadcast model of education to an interactive model, providing children with opportunities to interact with toys, craft materials, and other physical objects. But Froebel wasn't satisfied with the toys and materials that existed at the time. He set out to create new types of toys, designed specifically to support the goals of his new kindergarten.

In all, Froebel created a collection of 20 toys, which have become known as *Froebel's Gifts*. With Froebel's geometric tiles, children in his kindergarten could create mosaic patterns, like those found in parquet floors. With Froebel's blocks, children could build towers and buildings. With Froebel's colored papers, children could learn origami-style folding techniques for making shapes and patterns. With Froebel's sticks and peas, children could assemble three-dimensional structures.

All these activities were intended to give children an appreciation for the shapes, patterns, and symmetries of the natural world. Froebel wanted his kindergarten children to gain a better understanding of the world around them. One of the best ways to do that, he realized, was for children to create models of the world—to "re-create" the world through their own eyes, with their own hands. That was the ultimate goal of Froebel's Gifts: understanding through "re-creation."

Froebel also recognized the connection between *re-creation* and *recreation*. He understood that kindergarten children are most likely to create and build when they are engaged in playful, imaginative activities. So Froebel designed his Gifts to be structured and systematic but at the same time playful and engaging. Froebel's Gifts cross many boundaries, mixing art and design with science and engineering—and, in doing so, they provide an environment for engaging children in creative thinking and creative expression.

Froebel's ideas and his Gifts attracted great attention, first in Germany, then through Europe, and eventually in the United States. His work deeply influenced other educational theorists.

Maria Montessori built upon Froebel's ideas, particularly embracing the importance of engaging children's senses through physical, manipulative materials. The network of schools bearing Montessori's name owe a debt to Froebel and his ideas.

In his wonderful book *Inventing Kindergarten*, Norman Brosterman documents the influence of kindergarten—and, particularly, Froebel's Gifts—on culture and creativity in the 20th century. Many of the century's leading artists and designers pointed to their experiences in kindergarten as providing a foundation for their later creativity. Buckminster Fuller, for example, used Froebel's toothpicks and peas to experiment with triangular structures in kindergarten, and he later credited those early explorations as the underpinnings of his work on geodesic domes. Similarly, Frank Lloyd Wright said that his boyhood experiences with Froebel's Gifts served as a foundation for his architecture.

Makers of toys and educational manipulative materials also have been inspired by Froebel's ideas. Wooden blocks, LEGO bricks, Cuisenaire rods, pattern blocks, and Tinkertoys can all be viewed as descendants of Froebel's Gifts.

Froebel's influence can still be felt in many kindergartens around the world, but there are troubling trends. In many kindergartens today, children spend time filling out math worksheets and drilling with phonics flashcards. There's more focus on delivering early-literacy instruction and less time for playful exploration. Some people have referred to today's kindergartens as *literacy boot camps*.

On March 23, 2014, the *Washington Post* ran an article about a long-time kindergarten teacher, Susan Sluyter, who resigned her position. Sluyter explained her decision:

When I first began teaching more than 25 years ago, hands-on exploration, investigation, joy and love of learning characterized the early childhood classroom. I'd describe our current period as a time of testing, data collection, competition and punishment. One would be hard put these days to find joy present in classrooms. ...

There is a national push, related to the push for increased academics in early childhood classrooms, to cut play out of the kindergarten classroom. Many kindergartens across the country no longer have sand tables, block areas, drama areas and arts and crafts centers. This is a deeply ill-informed movement, as all early childhood experts continuously report that 4, 5 and 6 year olds learn largely through play.

In short, kindergarten is becoming like the rest of school. In this book, I argue for exactly the opposite: I believe the rest of school (indeed, the rest of life) should become more like kindergarten.

THE CREATIVE LEARNING SPIRAL

What's so special about the kindergarten approach to learning? Why do I think it's a good model for learners of all ages?

To get a better understanding of the kindergarten approach to learning, it's useful to think about a typical kindergarten activity. Imagine a group of kindergarten children, playing on the floor with a collection of wooden blocks. Two of the children begin building a castle, inspired by a fairy tale their teacher read to them. They build the base of the castle and then start building a lookout tower on top. They keep adding more blocks, and the tower gets taller and taller. Eventually, the tower tips over and falls to the ground. The children start building again, trying to make the tower more stable. Meanwhile, another child starts telling a story about the family living inside the castle. Her friend extends the story, adding a new character. The two children go back and forth, continually adding to the story. As the castle grows, so does the story.

As the kindergarten children play, they learn many things. As they build towers, they develop a better understanding of structures and stability. As they create stories, they develop a better understanding of plots and characters. Most important, they learn about the creative process, and they begin to develop as creative thinkers.

I like to think of the creative process in terms of a *Creative Learning Spiral*. As kindergarten children play with blocks, build castles, and tell stories, they engage with all aspects of the creative process:

Imagine: In our example, the children start by imagining a fantasy castle—and the family that lives inside.

Create: It's not enough to imagine. The children turn their ideas into action, creating a castle, a tower, a story.

Play: The children are constantly tinkering and experimenting with their creations, trying to build a taller tower or adding new twists and turns to the story.

Share: One group of children collaborates on building the castle, another group collaborates on creating the story, and the two groups share ideas with one another. Each new addition to the castle suggests a new story and vice versa.

Reflect: When the tower collapses, the teacher comes over and encourages the children to reflect on why it fell. How could they make a more stable tower? The teacher shows them pictures of skyscrapers, and the children notice that the bottoms of the buildings are wider than the tops. They decide to rebuild their tower with a wider base than before.

Imagine: Based on their experiences going through the spiral, the children imagine new ideas and new directions. How about creating a village around the castle? How about creating a puppet show about life in the village?

This Creative Learning Spiral is repeated over and over in kindergarten. The materials vary (wooden blocks, crayons, glitter, construction paper) and the creations vary (castles, stories, pictures, songs), but the core process is the same.

The Creative Learning Spiral is the engine of creative thinking. As kindergarten children go through the spiral, they develop and refine their abilities as creative thinkers. They learn to develop their own ideas, try them out, experiment with alternatives, get input from others, and generate new ideas based on their experiences.

Unfortunately, after kindergarten, most schools shift away from the Creative Learning Spiral. Students spend much of their time sitting at desks, filling out worksheets, and listening to lectures—whether from a teacher in the classroom or a video on the computer. Too often, schools focus on delivering instruction and information rather than supporting students in the creative learning process.

It doesn't need to be that way. In our graduate program at the MIT Media Lab, focused on creative uses of new technologies, we've adopted a kindergarten-like approach. Media Lab graduate students spend very little time in the classroom. Instead, they're constantly working on projects, guided by the Creative Learning Spiral. Students work on many different types of projects: Some design interactive musical instruments to support new forms of musical expression, while others develop prosthetic devices for people who lost their limbs. But the design process is similar in all cases. Students rapidly build prototypes, play with them, share their prototypes with other students, and reflect on what they've learned. Then, it's time to imagine the next version of the prototype, and they go through the spiral again—and again and again.

Of course, Media Lab students use very different tools and technologies than children in kindergarten. Media Lab students use microcontrollers and laser cutters more than finger paints and wooden blocks, but the Creative Learning Spiral is the same. The Media Lab is recognized around the world for its creativity and innovation, and I have no doubt that our project-based learning approach, based on the Creative Learning Spiral, provides the underpinning for this creativity.

The Creative Learning Spiral works in kindergartens and at the MIT Media Lab. How can we help it take root everywhere else?

GIVE P'S A CHANCE

In 2007, my research group at MIT launched the Scratch programming language. Over the past decade, tens of millions of children around the world have used Scratch to create their own interactive stories, games, and animations—and share their creations with one another in the Scratch online community (scratch.mit.edu).

One of the first children to try out Scratch, back in 2007, was an 11-year-old girl from California who signed up with the username MahoAshley. Her great passion was the Japanese art style known as *anime*, characterized by colorful graphics and vibrant characters. MahoAshley loved drawing anime characters, and she saw that Scratch provided a way to extend her work. Rather than just drawing anime characters, as she had done in the past, she could use Scratch to make her anime characters come to life. By snapping together combinations of Scratch programming blocks, MahoAshley could make her anime characters move, dance, talk, and sing.

MahoAshley started to program animated stories featuring her anime characters, and she shared her animations on the Scratch website. Other members of the Scratch community responded with great enthusiasm, posting glowing comments under her projects (such as "OMG I LUV IT!!!!!!"), along with questions about how she achieved certain visual effects (such as "How do you make a sprite look see-through?"). Encouraged, MahoAshley began to create and share Scratch projects on a regular basis, like episodes in a TV series. Her fans in the Scratch community eagerly awaited each new episode from MahoAshley.

Occasionally, MahoAshley would add new characters to her series. One day, she got an idea: Why not involve the whole Scratch community in the process? She created a Scratch project that announced a contest, asking other community members to design a sister for one of her characters. The project listed a set of requirements for the new character, including "Must have red or blue hair, please choose" and "Has to have either cat ears or ram horns, or a combo of both."

The project received more than 100 comments and dozens of submissions. One comment was from a community member who wanted to enter the contest but said she didn't know how to draw anime characters. So MahoAshley produced another Scratch project: a step-by-step tutorial, demonstrating a 13-step process for drawing and coloring anime characters.

Over the course of a year, MahoAshley programmed and shared more than 200 Scratch projects, covering a range of project types— stories, contests, tutorials, and more. Her programming and artistic skills progressed, and her projects clearly resonated with the Scratch community, receiving more than 12,000 comments.

Before using Scratch, MahoAshley had never created a computer program. As she worked with Scratch, she was clearly learning new computer science concepts and skills. But in my mind, that's not what was most important about MahoAshley's Scratch experiences. For me, what was most impressive was the way MahoAshley was developing as a creative thinker. She was continually cycling through the Creative Learning Spiral: imagining, creating, playing, sharing, reflecting, and then imagining again.

MahoAshley was learning how to navigate a new and unfamiliar environment. She was learning how to transform her ideas into projects—and to experiment with new types of projects. She was learning how to collaborate with others and how to adapt her work based on feedback from others. These are all attributes of a creative thinker.

How can we encourage and support these types of creative learning experiences? In my research group at MIT, we've developed a set of four guiding principles for helping young people develop as creative thinkers: projects, passion, peers, and play. In short, we believe the best way to cultivate creativity is to support people working on *projects* based on their *passions*, in collaboration with *peers* and in a *playful* spirit.

Our continuing development of Scratch is guided by these *four P's of creative learning*:

Projects: Creating projects is the central activity in the Scratch community. As MahoAshley worked with Scratch, she was continually creating projects—and continually going through the Creative Learning Spiral, developing a deeper understanding of the creative process.

Passion: When people work on projects they care about, they're willing to work longer and harder. Because Scratch supports many different types of projects (games, stories, animations, and more), everyone can work on projects they care about. In the case of MahoAshley, she could create projects connected to her passion for anime—and also work on new types of projects (contests and tutorials) as new ideas emerged.

Peers: Creativity is a social process, with people collaborating, sharing, and building on one another's work. By integrating programming with an online community, Scratch is designed for social interaction. MahoAshley took full advantage of the social side of Scratch, sharing her expertise with the community (via tutorials) and asking other community members for input (via contests and comments).

Play: Scratch is designed to support playful experimentation as a pathway to creativity, encouraging young people to take risks and try new things. MahoAshley embraced this playful spirit, continually experimenting with new types of projects and new ways of interacting with the community.

These four P's don't represent radically new ideas; they build on decades of work by many researchers around the world. But I find the four P's to be a valuable framework for guiding my work. In my research group, we constantly think about projects, passion, peers, and play as we develop new technologies and new activities.

And the four P's aren't just for university researchers. They can serve as a useful framework for teachers, parents, and anyone else interested in supporting creative learning. That's why I've organized the core chapters of this book around the four P's.

With apologies to John Lennon: All we are saying is give P's a chance.

WHAT CREATIVITY IS—AND ISN'T

Not everyone agrees on the value and importance of creative thinking in today's society. Part of the problem is that there is no consensus on what it means to be creative. Different people think about creativity in very different ways, so it's not surprising that they can't agree on its value and importance. As I've talked with people about creativity, I've encountered a number of common misconceptions.

MISCONCEPTION #1: CREATIVITY IS ABOUT ARTISTIC EXPRESSION

We value and admire painters, sculptors, and poets for their creativity. But other types of people can be creative too. Scientists can be creative when they develop new theories. Doctors can be creative when they diagnose diseases. Entrepreneurs can be creative when they develop new products. Social workers can be creative when they suggest strategies for struggling families. Politicians can be creative when they develop new policies.

I believe that the common association of creativity with artistic expression contributes to an undervaluing of creativity in the minds of many parents. When I talk with parents about creativity, they often assume that I'm talking about artistic expression. Because most parents don't put a high priority on how well their children can express themselves artistically, they say that it would be "nice" for their children to be creative, but they don't see it as essential. To sidestep this line of thinking, I often use the phrase *creative thinking* rather than *creativity*. When parents hear *creative thinking*, they're less likely to focus on artistic expression and more likely to see it as something essential for their children's future.

MISCONCEPTION #2: ONLY A SMALL SEGMENT
OF THE POPULATION IS CREATIVE

Some people feel that the words *creative* and *creativity* should be used only when referring to inventions and ideas that are totally new to the world. In this view, winners of Nobel Prizes are creative, and artists whose works are on display at major museums are creative, but not the rest of us.

Researchers who study creativity sometimes refer to this type of creativity as *Big-C Creativity*. I'm more interested in what researchers call *little-c creativity*. When you come up with an idea that's useful to you in your everyday life, that's little-c creativity. It doesn't matter if thousands—or millions—of people came up with similar ideas in the past. If the idea is new and useful to you, it's little-c creativity.

The invention of the paper clip was Big-C Creativity; every time someone comes up with a new way to use a paper clip in everyday life, that's little-c creativity.

Sometimes, educators focus too much attention on Big-C Creativity and not enough on little-c creativity. A few years ago, I made a presentation about creativity to a group of educators. In the Q&A session at the end, one educator said that it was very important for us to develop better methods for assessing creativity so that we could identify those students with the greatest capacity to be creative. In my mind, that's exactly the wrong view. Everyone can be (little-c) creative, and we need to help everyone reach their full creative potential.

MISCONCEPTION #3: CREATIVITY COMES IN A FLASH OF INSIGHT

Popular stories about creativity often revolve around an *Aha! moment*. Archimedes shouted "Eureka!" in the bathtub when he realized that he could calculate the volume of irregularly shaped objects by submerging them in water (and measuring the amount of water displaced). Isaac Newton recognized the universal nature of gravitational force when he was sitting beneath an apple tree—and was hit on the head by a falling apple. August Kekule realized the structure of the benzene ring after daydreaming about a snake eating its tail.

But such Aha! moments, if they exist at all, are just a small part of the creative process. Most scientists, inventors, and artists recognize that creativity is a long-term process. Constantin Brancusi, one of the pioneers of modernist art, wrote: "Being creative is not being hit by a lightning bolt from God. It's having clear intent and passion." Thomas Edison famously said that creativity is 1 percent inspiration and 99 percent perspiration.

But what is the person doing while perspiring? What type of activity precedes the Aha! moment? It's not just a matter of hard work. Creativity grows out of a certain type of hard work, combining curious exploration with playful experimentation and systematic investigation. New ideas and insights might seem like they come in a flash, but they usually happen after many cycles of imagining, creating, playing, sharing, and reflecting—that is, after many iterations through the Creative Learning Spiral.

MISCONCEPTION #4: YOU CAN'T TEACH CREATIVITY

There's no doubt that babies come into the world full of curiosity. They want to touch, to interact, to explore, to understand. As they grow older, they want to express themselves: to talk, to sing, to draw, to build, to dance.

Some people think that the best way to support children's creativity is to get out of their way: You shouldn't try to teach creativity; just stand back and let children's natural curiosity take over.

I have some sympathy with this point of view. It's true that the rigid structures of some schools and some homes can squelch children's curiosity and creativity. I also agree that you can't teach creativity, if *teach* means giving children a clear set of rules and instructions on how to be creative.

But you can *nurture* creativity. All children are born with the capacity to be creative, but their creativity won't necessarily develop on its own. It needs to be nurtured, encouraged, supported. The process is like that of a farmer or gardener taking care of plants by creating an environment in which the plants will flourish. Similarly, you can create a learning environment in which creativity will flourish.

So, yes, you *can* teach creativity, so long as you think about *teaching* as an organic, interactive process. Indeed, that's what this book is all about.

TENSIONS AND TRADE-OFFS: TECHNOLOGY

It's not easy to cultivate creativity in schools and homes. Even when educators and parents recognize and appreciate the value of creative thinking, they face many tensions and trade-offs when trying to implement strategies to encourage and support it. So, throughout this book, I'm including sections that explore some of these tensions and trade-offs. For this opening chapter, I'll focus on the role of new technologies in children's learning.

Discussions about new technologies have become increasingly polarized. On one side are people who might be called *techno-enthusiasts*; they tend to get excited about the possibilities of almost all new technologies—the newer, the better. On the other side are people who might be called *techno-skeptics*; they worry about the negative impacts of new technologies. They prefer that children spend more time with traditional toys and outdoor play and less time on screens.

I get frustrated by both sides. Let me explain why—and explore how we might think about things differently.

Let's start with the techno-enthusiasts. With digital technologies playing an increasingly important role in all parts of the culture and economy, it's hardly surprising that people are enthusiastic about using new technologies to enhance learning and education. And with children spending more and more time playing games on their phones, tablets, and computers, it's hardly surprising that educators are trying to integrate gaming into classroom activities, hoping to leverage the high level of motivation and engagement that children exhibit when playing games.

There is a certain logic to all of this—but there's a problem. Too often, designers of educational materials and activities simply add a thin layer of technology and gaming over antiquated curriculum and pedagogy, somewhat like putting lipstick on a pig.

In one classroom I visited, there was a large display at the front of the room, and each student had a network-connected laptop. The teacher asked questions, and the students entered responses on their laptops. On the large display, for all to see, was a listing of which students had answered the question correctly, and how quickly each student had responded. Students were awarded points based on their speed and accuracy, and the display showed a running tally of their scores.

The software was well-designed, and the teacher was happy to have easy access to well-organized data on student performance. I have no doubt that some of the students found this game-like approach very motivating. But I'm also sure that some students found it very discouraging and disempowering. And the activity put an emphasis on questions that can be answered quickly with right and wrong answers—certainly not the type of questions that I would prioritize in a classroom.

The activity reminded me of my own experiences in fourth grade, when the teacher rearranged the order of our desks each Monday based on our scores on the previous Friday's spelling test. I believe that this highly visible weekly ranking was bad for all students— those in the first row as well as those in the last. It was painful for me to see the same pedagogical approach repeated decades later, with greater efficiency, thanks to new technologies.

As frustrated as I get with techno-enthusiasts, I get equally frustrated with techno-skeptics. In many cases, the skeptics apply very different standards to new technologies than to "old" technologies. They worry about the antisocial impact of a child spending hours working on a computer, but they don't seem to have any concerns about a child spending the same time reading a book. They worry that children interacting with computers don't spend enough time outside, but they don't voice similar concerns about children playing musical instruments. I'm not suggesting that there are no reasons for concern. I'm just asking for more consistency.

When digital technologies started to enter the lives of children, an organization called the Alliance for Childhood published a report called *Fool's Gold: A Critical Look at Computers in Childhood*. The report argued that "low-tech tools like crayons, watercolors, and paper nourish children's inner capacities and encourage the child to freely move in, directly relate to, and understand the real world." I agree with this—but the same can be true for high-tech tools. Can't building and programming a robotic sculpture "nourish children's inner capacities" too?

People tend to forget that crayons and watercolors were viewed as "advanced technologies" at some point in the past. We see them differently now because they've become integrated into the culture. Computer pioneer Alan Kay likes to say that technology is anything that was invented after you were born. For kids growing up today, laptops and mobile phones aren't high-tech tools—they're everyday tools, just like crayons and watercolors.

I think I become particularly aggravated with techno-skeptics not because I *disagree* with them on so many things, but rather because I *agree* with them on so many things. Most techno-skeptics have goals and values very similar to my own. Most of them are deeply committed to providing children with opportunities to develop their imagination and creativity. Because we're so aligned in our goals and values, I really want them to see new technologies the same way that I do, to see the possibilities for expanding children's creative thinking and creative expression. But when techno-skeptics look at new technologies, they seem to see only the challenges, not the possibilities.

Today, concerns about the role of new technologies in children's lives are often expressed in terms of *screen time*. Parents and teachers are trying to decide if they should set limits on how much time their children spend interacting with screens. I think this debate misses the point. Of course there's a problem if children spend all their time interacting with screens—just as there would be a problem if they spent all their time playing the violin or reading books or playing sports. Spending all your time on any one thing is problematic. But the most important issue with screen time is not quantity but quality. There are many ways of interacting with screens; it doesn't make sense to treat them all the same. Time spent playing a violent video game is different from time spent texting with friends, which is different from time spent researching a report for school, which is different from time spent creating a Scratch project.

Rather than trying to minimize screen time, I think parents and teachers should try to maximize creative time. The focus shouldn't be on which technologies children are using, but rather what children are doing with them. Some uses of new technologies foster creative thinking; others restrict it. The same is true for older technologies. Rather than trying to choose between high-tech, low-tech, and no-tech, parents and teachers should be searching for activities that will engage children in creative thinking and creative expression.

IN THEIR OWN VOICES: TARYN

To understand the value and possibilities of lifelong kindergarten, it is important to hear directly from the young people who are experiencing it, so I'm ending each chapter with an interview with someone who grew up engaged with technologies and projects from my MIT research group. The first interview features Taryn, a 16-year-old in South Africa, who has been a long-time member of the Scratch online community, where she's known as bubble103.

Me: How did you get started with Scratch?

Taryn: It started as one lesson in a computer class at my school, when I was 10 years old. It was only one lesson, and we were told: put blocks in order, do this, do that. I didn't really like it that much. I tried playing with Scratch at home. The first thing that I made myself, my 10-year-old self, was an animation of a baby flying in a box. But I couldn't get it to work, so I stopped playing with it.

Then, a year later, I saw my friend making a game out of Scratch. I asked, "How did you do that?" and then it all started. That was my first collaboration. We'd sit this old laptop on a bed and start making things and grabbing the mouse from each other; it was so much fun. It's one of my best memories.

I signed up for an account on the website when I was 12. I had been watching from afar—going, wow, there's cool stuff happening, but I'm not sure I'm brave enough to go join, because I'm a really shy person. Joining the community was the best thing I ever did. When I first shared a project online, I didn't expect anyone to see it or anything. I just wanted to figure out how to share projects. Then I got a comment; I can't even remember what it was, I just remember how it made me feel, like "Someone just talked to me! They liked my project!" It was amazing to get feedback from people that I'd never met. So I started making more projects: a Halloween spooky castle, a farming game, a tour of Venus.

I've just been constantly blown away by the kind of support and collaboration and sharing that happens in the community. That's one of the main things that keeps me coming back to Scratch every day. It's so inspiring. There are so many opportunities to learn from other people in the community. People are doing things that I didn't even think could be possible.

Me: While you've been learning from others, you've also been sharing what you've learned. I know you've created a few tutorials in Scratch, including one called *You Gotta Love Variables*.

Taryn: I love teaching, and I love thinking of new ways to explain things or think about things. As I was working on a Scratch project,

I figured out some things about variables that I hadn't known before, and I was really excited about it, and I didn't know what to do with that feeling besides share it. So I created a Scratch project to help other Scratchers learn about variables.

I love it when people comment that they learned something new from the tutorial. I know how wonderful it feels when you figure out something, like, "Yes!" The idea that I could give that feeling to someone else was, like, mind equals blown. I was nervous about talking to people or teaching people face-to-face, so the idea that I could still spread my experiences and my knowledge without having to face that kind of social fear was amazing and really freeing.

Me: You're best known in the Scratch community for a series of projects called *Colour Divide*. How did you get started on that?

Taryn: It started as a collaboration with five other Scratchers. We were role-playing in a Scratch studio, coming up with a story about a fantasy city. We were just having fun role-playing and getting to know each other. But then I got struck by inspiration. I was like, "I need to animate this." I hadn't ever animated before, but that didn't matter because I was inspired. I'd been working with the Scratch environment for long enough that I felt comfortable enough to just try it. I felt like I was a storyteller who could use programming to make her story come alive. The story was driving me forward, and the ideas I had were driving me forward.

Colour Divide is set in a fantasy dystopian world where kids are subjected to one test that determines their place in society. Everyone is ranked based on their magical ability. If they're not so good at magic, that's a level red. The most powerful are violet. If they're not strong enough to get even a red, they're banished to the wilderness. The story centers around the characters that don't quite fit into this mold and end up challenging this society, and the whole story is about them discovering where they fit and how to change things for the better.

Me: I know the story has special meaning for you, growing up in South Africa.

Taryn: A lot of the story is me making sense of the world where I've grown up and things I've seen around me. Growing up, I've definitely seen the scars that apartheid has left on my country and the people. I'm really exploring that through the different characters that are a part of this story. The divide is a euphemism for any kind of divide. It's saying, "You're not defined by one small part of you. You are a person that is so much bigger than this one little piece that society has decided for you." That's the message that I really feel strongly about and I wanted to share.

Society has a lot of labels that are being pushed to stick on you. But people are so much more complex and beautiful and amazing than that. For me, it's definitely linked to my experience with Scratch—it's totally a place where all kinds of people come together, introverts and extroverts, arts and programming, mushing together. For me, who never felt I fit into any one thing, what I love most about Scratch is all of those things coming together.

Me: What was the reaction from the Scratch community when you published *Colour Divide*?

Taryn: My first *Colour Divide* project was just a trailer. Lots of Scratchers encouraged me to do more episodes—and they offered to help. They were like, "I want to be in this too. I want to make a character for this." So I started to get more and more people involved. I set it up so that other Scratchers could contribute faces and voices and scenery and music. It felt less like something that I was making, more like something that we were making together.

Most of the voice actors are people from other ends of the world that I've never met before, and I worked with them to bring the characters to life with their voices. All the music is made by other Scratchers. I'm inspired by how they share their music on Scratch, just for other Scratchers to use. Most of the background characters, like the faces in the scenery in the episodes, are all designed by the Scratchers. We're all in this world together.

Me: Looking back over the past six years, what are the biggest ways that you've changed because of Scratch?

Taryn: Because of Scratch, I've become more confident to try new things and express myself—and more comfortable with taking risks and making mistakes. As someone who has always been paralyzed by a fear of making mistakes, programming in Scratch has just changed the way that I see that. It's really empowered me when I'm doing creative work and just generally in my life. Now, when something goes wrong, I see it as an opportunity to learn something new.

That to me is creative confidence. That's the kind of people that Scratch is growing, and I honestly think Scratchers are going to change the world, seriously.

PROJECTS

MAKERS OF THINGS

In January 2009, in a large lecture hall on the MIT campus, I watched Barack Obama inaugurated as the 44th president of the United States. The room was packed with more than 500 people, and a video of Obama's inauguration speech was projected on two large screens at the front of the room. Given that the audience was full of MIT scientists and engineers, you won't be surprised to hear that the strongest reaction came when Obama declared: "We'll restore science to its rightful place." The room erupted with applause.

But that's not the line in the inaugural address that captured my attention. For me, the most memorable moment was when Obama said: "It has been the risk-takers, the doers, the makers of things— some celebrated, but more often men and women obscure in their labor—who have carried us up the long, rugged path towards prosperity and freedom."

Risk-takers. Doers. Makers of things. These are the X students, the creative thinkers. They've been the driving force for economic, technological, political, and cultural change throughout history. Today, everyone needs to be a risk-taker, a doer, a maker of things—not necessarily to bend the arc of history, but to bend the arcs of their own lives.

By using the phrase *makers of things*, Obama was making an implicit reference to a movement that was just starting to spread through our culture: the Maker Movement. It started as a grass-roots movement, in basements, garages, and community centers, among people who had a passion for making things—and sharing their ideas and creations with one another. In 2005, the movement gained momentum when Dale Dougherty launched *Make:* magazine, celebrating the joys of building, creating, and inventing things. The magazine aimed to democratize making, showing how everyone can get involved in do-it-yourself activities. The first issue described "amazing things that ordinary people are making in their garages and backyards," providing instructions for making a kite to take aerial photographs, a thermoelectric keg wrap to keep beer cold, and glow sticks to make dynamic light patterns at night.

The following year, in 2006, Dale organized the first Maker Faire, described as a "family-friendly festival of invention, creativity, and resourcefulness." There were exhibits and workshops for making jewelry, making furniture, making robots—making almost anything you could imagine. Over the past decade, hundreds of Maker Faires have sprung up around the world, attracting millions of engineers, artists, designers, entrepreneurs, educators, parents, and children.

For many people, the appeal of the Maker Movement is in the technology. There has been a proliferation of new technologies, such as 3-D printers and laser cutters, that enable people to design, produce, and customize physical objects. Many people are excited about the business potential of these technologies, predicting that the Maker Movement will spark a new industrial revolution, in which small businesses (or even individuals) can manufacture products that previously required large factories with economies of scale.

I'm attracted to the Maker Movement for different reasons. I believe the it has the potential to be not just a technological and economic movement but also a learning movement, providing new ways for people to engage in creative learning experiences. As people make and create, they have opportunities to develop as creative thinkers. After all, *create* is at the root of *creativity*.

Perhaps most important, the Maker Movement encourages people to work on projects—the first of the four P's of creative learning. The articles in *Make:* magazine and the exhibits at Maker Faire don't just teach the techniques of making; they support a project-based approach to learning, in which people learn new ideas, skills, and strategies while working on personally meaningful projects. Dale Dougherty refers to projects as "the basic units of making."

I experienced the power of projects in a personal way as I was growing up. As a child, I enjoyed playing all types of sports: baseball, basketball, tennis, and more. But even more than playing sports, I enjoyed "making" sports. I was constantly inventing new sports to play with my brother and my cousin. I was fortunate to have a backyard for building and playing—and fortunate to have parents who allowed me to turn the backyard into a workspace for my projects.

One summer, I dug up the backyard to create my own miniature golf course. It was a continual learning experience. I started by digging simple holes in the ground for the golf holes, but I found that the holes lost their shape over time, so I began embedding aluminum cans in the holes. That worked fine until it rained, and the cans filled up with water that was difficult to get rid of. My solution: cut off both ends of the cans before embedding them in the ground so that water could drain out of the bottom.

As I added walls and obstacles on the mini-golf course, I needed to figure out how the ball would ricochet off of them. That provided me with a motivating context for learning the physics of collisions.

I spent hours calculating and measuring angles so that I could bounce a golf ball off obstacles and into the hole. That experience was more memorable than any science lesson I had in the classroom.

Along the way, I began to develop an understanding about not only the process for making a miniature golf course, but the general process for making anything: how to start with an initial idea, develop preliminary plans, create a first version, try it out, ask other people to try it out, revise plans based on what happens—and keep doing that, over and over. By working on my project, I was gaining experience with the Creative Learning Spiral.

Through these types of projects, I began to see myself as someone who could make and create things. I started to look at things in the world in a new way, wondering how they were made. How is a golf ball made, or a golf club? I started to wonder what other things I could make.

If you search on the *Make:* website today (makezine.com), you'll find lots of articles describing miniature golf projects, with titles like "DIY Tabletop Mini Golf" and "Urban Putt: Miniature Golf 2.0." The technologies have evolved since I built my miniature golf course nearly 50 years ago. It's now possible to produce custom-designed obstacles with a 3-D printer or laser cutter, and it's now possible to embed sensors in the obstacles, triggering motors or LEDs to turn on as the golf ball careens off an obstacle.

I'm still proud of the "old-fashioned" miniature golf course that I built as a child. But I'm also excited that new technologies can expand the types of projects that children can create—and inspire more children to become makers of things.

LEARNING THROUGH MAKING

Over the years, many educators and researchers have advocated *learning by doing*, arguing that people learn best when they are actively involved in *doing* things, learning through hands-on activities.

But in the culture of the Maker Movement, it's not enough to *do* something: You need to *make* something. According to the maker ethic, the most valuable learning experiences come when you're actively engaged in designing, building, or creating something—when you're *learning through making*.

If you want to get a better understanding of the connections between making and learning, and how to support learning through making, there is no better place to look than the work of Seymour Papert. I was lucky enough to work with Seymour for many years at MIT. More than anyone else, Seymour developed the intellectual foundations for learning through making, along with compelling technologies and strategies for supporting it. Indeed, Seymour should be considered the patron saint of the Maker Movement.

Seymour loved learning in all of its dimensions: understanding it, supporting it, doing it. After earning a PhD in mathematics from Cambridge University in 1959, Seymour moved to Geneva to work with the great Swiss psychologist Jean Piaget. Through careful observation and interviews with thousands of children, Piaget found that children actively construct knowledge through their everyday interactions with people and objects in the world. Knowledge isn't poured into children, like water into a vase. Instead, children are constantly creating, revising, and testing their own theories about the world as they play with their toys and friends. According to

Piaget's *constructivist* theory of learning, children are active builders of knowledge, not passive recipients. Children don't *get* ideas, they *make* ideas.

In the early 1960s, Seymour moved from Geneva, Switzerland, to Cambridge, Massachusetts, to take a faculty position at MIT. In doing so, Seymour was moving from the epicenter of a revolution in child development to the epicenter of a revolution in computing technology—and he spent the following decades making connections between the two revolutions. When Seymour arrived at MIT, computers still cost hundreds of thousands of dollars or more, and they were used only at large companies, government agencies, and universities. But Seymour foresaw that computers would eventually become accessible for everyone, even children, and he had a vision for how computing could transform the ways children learn and play.

Seymour soon emerged as a leader in a spirited intellectual battle over how to introduce computers in education. Most researchers and educators adopted a *computer-aided instruction* approach, in which computers played the role of teachers: delivering information and instruction to students, conducting quizzes to measure what the students had learned, then adapting subsequent instruction based on student responses to the quiz questions.

Seymour had a radically different vision. For Seymour, computers were not a replacement for the teacher but a new medium of expression, a new tool for making things. In 1971, still five years before the first personal computer was introduced, Seymour coauthored (with Cynthia Solomon) an article titled "Twenty Things to Do with a Computer." The article described how children could use computers to draw pictures, create games, control robots, compose music, and many other creative activities.

Seymour's approach built on what he had learned from Piaget, viewing children as active constructors, not passive recipients, of knowledge. Seymour went a step further, arguing that children construct knowledge most effectively when they are actively involved in constructing things in the world—that is, when they are makers of things. Seymour called his approach *constructionism*, because it brings together two types of construction: As children construct things in the world, they construct new ideas in their heads, which motivates them to construct new things in the world, and on and on, in a never-ending spiral of learning.

To bring these ideas to life, Seymour and his colleagues developed a computer programming language for children, called *Logo*. Until then, programming had been viewed as a specialized activity, accessible only to people with advanced mathematical backgrounds. But Seymour saw programming as a universal language for making things on the computer, and he argued that everyone should learn to program.

In his book *Mindstorms*, Seymour contrasted the computer-aided instruction approach, in which "the computer is being used to program the child," with his own approach, in which "the child programs the computer." In the process of learning to program, he wrote, a child "both acquires a sense of mastery over a piece of the most modern and powerful technology and establishes an intimate contact with some of the deepest ideas from science, from mathematics, and from the art of intellectual model building."

When Logo was first developed, children used it primarily for controlling the motions of a robotic "turtle" (so named because it used a hemispherical shell to protect its electronics). As personal computers became available in the late 1970s, children used Logo to draw pictures on the screen, typing commands like "forward 100" and "right 60" to tell the "screen turtle" how to move, turn, and draw. As children wrote Logo programs, they learned mathematical ideas in a meaningful and motivating way, in the context of working on projects they cared about.

Through the 1980s, thousands of schools taught millions of students how to program in Logo, but the initial enthusiasm didn't last. Many teachers and students had difficulty learning to program in Logo, because the language was full of nonintuitive syntax and punctuation. To make matters worse, Logo was often introduced through activities that didn't sustain the interest of either teachers or students. Many classrooms taught Logo as an end unto itself, not as a way for students to express themselves and to explore what Seymour called "powerful ideas." Before long, most schools shifted to other uses for computers. They began to see computers as tools for delivering and accessing information, not for making and creating as Seymour had imagined.

Seymour's ideas about learning through making are now starting to gain traction once again, as evidenced by the rise of the Maker Movement. Although Seymour's work on Logo began more than 50 years ago and his landmark book *Mindstorms* was published back in 1980, his core ideas are as important and pertinent today as ever before.

TOYS TO THINK WITH

The first feature-length computer-animated film, *Toy Story*, was released in 1995. It was both a commercial and critical success, widely recognized as one of the best animated films of all time.

Many of the key scenes in *Toy Story* take place in two children's bedrooms. Andy's room is full of toys that talk and interact with one another. Mr. Potato Head, Little Bo Peep, Slinky Dog, and many other popular toys come to life in Andy's bedroom. The center of attention is Buzz Lightyear, the newest high-tech toy of the year ("a member of the elite Universe Protection Unit of the Space Ranger Corps").

Sid's bedroom, across the backyard, feels more like an inventor's workshop than a bedroom, filled with not only toys but also screwdrivers, hammers, and other tools. Sid is constantly taking apart his toys and recombining them in unexpected ways. Sid isn't just playing with toys, he is making toys.

Andy's room is clearly intended to represent every child's dream, full of intelligent toys that interact and respond on their own. But I think it's Sid, the maker of things, who is more likely to develop as a creative thinker.

Unfortunately, movies often portray young makers like Sid in a negative light. In Toy Story, Sid's bedroom is presented as a dark and sinister place. Sid's creative abilities are mixed together with psychopathic behavior. At one point, Sid removes the head of flying lizard and transplants it onto his sister's favorite doll—"a double bypass brain transplant," he proclaims proudly.

When you walk into a toy store these days, it feels as if you've walked into Andy's room. All the toys are ready to interact and communicate. Stroke the back of a toy dinosaur, and it wags its tail in appreciation. Start talking to the dinosaur, and it talks back.

Today's technology is amazing. Toys are filled with electronics and sensors that can detect movements, gestures, and sounds, then respond with lights, music, and motion. As electronic components continue to become smaller and cheaper, more and more computational power is being packed into toys. But what are children learning as they interact with these toys? I have no doubt that the engineers and designers at the toy companies are learning a great deal when they create these toys, but what about the children who interact with the toys? Just because a toy itself is creative doesn't mean that it will help children become creative.

How can you decide which toys are best for your children? Here's my advice: *Ask not what the toy can do for your child; ask what your child can do with the toy.* When I see a new toy, I want to know what types of play the toy supports and encourages. If kids can use the toy to imagine and create their own projects, immersing themselves in the Creative Learning Spiral, then I'm excited about it. Rather than *toys that think*, I'm interested in *toys to think with*.

That's why I've always been attracted to LEGO bricks. The LEGO brick was invented specifically to provide children with new opportunities to imagine, create, and share. Children around the world use LEGO bricks to build houses, towers, castles, spaceships, and a wide variety of other creations—and, in doing so, they develop their abilities to think creatively, reason systematically, and work collaboratively.

The LEGO brick served as inspiration for the first project I worked on with Seymour Papert, shortly after I arrived at MIT in 1983. At the time, Seymour's Logo programming language was spreading to schools around the world. A few of us on Seymour's team (Steve Ocko, Brian Silverman, and myself) began exploring ways to connect LEGO bricks with Logo, so that children could write Logo computer programs to control their LEGO creations. We called the combined system *LEGO/Logo*.

In one of our early workshops, for example, a fifth-grade girl named Fran built a LEGO elevator, including a LEGO motor that pulled a string to make the elevator move up and down. She wrote a Logo program that turned the motor on for different amounts of time, to make the elevator move between floors. Later, Fran added a touch sensor at the top of the elevator, and she updated the Logo program so that the elevator would change direction automatically when it reached the top floor.

LEGO/Logo projects provided children with multiple opportunities for learning through making, by combining two different types of making: making LEGO models and making Logo programs. As Fran made her LEGO elevator, she learned about structures, mechanisms, and sensors; as she made her Logo program, she learned about sequencing, conditionals, and feedback. Perhaps most important, she learned about the process of creating her own project, from initial idea to working prototype.

The LEGO Group introduced LEGO/Logo as a product in 1988. Soon after that, a group of us at MIT (including Fred Martin and Randy Sargent) started working on the next generation of the technology. With LEGO/Logo, children used cables to connect their LEGO models to personal computers; for example, Fran used a cable to connect her LEGO elevator to an Apple II computer. As electronics continued to become smaller, we realized that we could pack computer capabilities inside a (large) LEGO brick. With this "programmable brick," children could build computational power directly into their LEGO constructions, rather than tethering their creations to an external computer.

As we began testing programmable bricks with children, we were delighted to see what they created. In one elementary-school class, children built a robotic zoo, with many types of programmable creatures. In another class, a child built a machine that automatically watered her plants, using a sensor to measure the dryness of the soil and a motorized mechanism to tilt the watering can.

The LEGO Group turned our programmable brick prototypes into its LEGO Mindstorms product (named after Seymour's classic book *Mindstorms*). Today, millions of children (and lots of adult hobbyists, too) use Mindstorms kits to build and program their own robotic inventions. In every country around the world, there are now robot competitions in which children build robots to navigate around obstacles, pick up objects, and solve other tasks.

The robotic inventions that children create with LEGO Mindstorms kits generally are not as sophisticated or as "smart" as the prepackaged robotic toys available in toy stores—just as the toys that Sid created in his bedroom were not as sophisticated as the anthropomorphic toys in Andy's bedroom. But the children who grow up making, creating, and inventing are the ones who will be better prepared for life in tomorrow's society.

CREATIVITY ON THE SCREEN

Just as today's toy stores are full of computerized toys that are wonderfully creative but don't give children much opportunity to create, the situation is similar with children's apps, video games, and online activities.

Children around the world are spending more and more time on the screen: playing video games, texting with friends, watching videos, searching for information. The technologies underlying these activities, like those in the toy store, are wonderfully creative.

But in most of these activities, children are only *interacting* with the technologies, not *creating* with them. If we want children to grow up as creative thinkers, we need to provide them with different ways of engaging on the screen, providing them with more opportunities to create their own projects and express their own ideas.

Let me share an example. A few years ago, I was invited to make a presentation at a conference called *Story 3.0*. The conference focused on "the innovation, culture, and business of next-generation storytelling," examining how digital technologies could transform the nature and role of stories in the 21st century, just as previous technologies (like the printing press and photography) had transformed storytelling in earlier eras. I was asked to speak about my research group's work on Scratch, which can be viewed as a 21st-century version of Seymour Papert's Logo programming language.

I was scheduled to speak the first morning of the conference. The speaker immediately before me was from an educational publishing company in Europe that was developing an immersive online world based on *Warriors*, a popular series of children's books that follow the adventures of four clans of wild cats in their forest homes. The publishing company hoped to leverage the popularity of the *Warriors* books to engage children in new forms of online interaction. The idea was for each child to play the role of one of the Warrior cats as part of a larger online story. As the speaker described in his presentation: "There will be hundreds of other cats in this forest with you ... What will happen is that you will consume these narrative missions, and each mission is presented as an essential piece of the clan's mythology that you need to grasp."

As I listened to the presentation, one word jumped out at me: *consume*. The publishing company saw online technologies as a new way to deliver stories for children to consume. Of course, children would not just sit passively in this online story. Part of the attraction of the online world is the ability to interact. In this case, children could move their virtual cats around the online world in order to solve the missions presented to them. But children would still be consumers: They would be interacting with someone else's story.

This product was a stark contrast to our Scratch software, which provides children with opportunities not only to interact with other people's stories but to create and share their own. I wondered if children were using Scratch to make their own stories based on the *Warriors* books. As the publishing company representative continued his presentation, I opened my laptop, went to the Scratch website, and typed "warrior cats" in the search box. A list with hundreds of projects and galleries appeared. One gallery called "BEST WARRIOR CATS PROJECTS!" had 150 projects. Another called "Warrior cat games and makers" had more than 70 projects. "Warrior Cats Rule!" had more than 60.

I looked at some of the projects, hoping to integrate a few of them into my presentation. I opened a project called *Warrior Cats Maker*, created by a Scratcher with the username Emberclaw. With this project, you can create your own Warrior cat. By pressing different buttons, you can select the length of the cat's fur (3 options), the color of the fur (16 options), the pattern of spots on the fur (11 options), the type of eyes (10 options), and the environment where the cat lives (4 options).

Next, I tried a project called *Warrior Cats Game v2*, created by a Scratcher with the username Flamespirit. In the game, you can use the arrow keys to move a cat through a series of environments, interacting (and fighting) with other cats along the way. You can press different keys to execute different fighting moves (such as back kick and claw attack) or click on plants in the environment to get information about their medicinal value. More than 1,500 members of the Scratch community had played *Warrior Cats Game v2*, and they left more than 100 comments and suggestions.

I quickly revised my presentation to include some of the *Warriors* projects from the Scratch community. When it was my turn to present, I emphasized the differences between the online *Warriors* world (featured in the previous presentation) and the Scratch online community. For me, the two initiatives represent two very different approaches to storytelling with online technologies—and, more broadly, very different approaches to education and learning. In one case, children are interacting with digital technologies, participating in someone else's story. In the other case, children are creating with digital technologies, telling their own stories.

With Scratch, children are always thinking in terms of projects. They are continually asking themselves: What type of project should I make? How can I improve it? What should I share with others? How should I respond to their comments and suggestions?

In many ways, Scratch is the digital equivalent of the LEGO construction kit. With LEGO bricks, children build their own houses and castles, rather than simply playing with premade houses and castles. With Scratch, children program their own stories and games, rather than simply interacting with premade stories and games.

I've always loved the LEGO slogan: "Joy of Building, Pride of Creation." I think it captures why LEGO bricks have been so successful—and why they've become a symbol of creative play and creative thinking. With Scratch, our goal is to bring "Joy of Building, Pride of Creation" to the online world, providing children with new ways to "build" (programming interactive stories and games), new ways to share their creations (in an online community), and new ways to develop as creative thinkers.

FLUENCY

In the past few years, there has been a surge of interest in learning computer programming—or coding, as it's popularly called these days. There are now thousands of apps, websites, and workshops to help kids learn to code. Our Scratch programming software is part of this trend—but with a distinct difference.

Most introductions to coding are based on *puzzles*. Kids are asked to create a program to move a virtual character past some obstacles to reach a goal. For example, move the *Star Wars* robot BB-8 to pick up scrap metal without running into the bandit, or program R2-D2 to get a message to the rebel pilots. As kids create programs to solve these puzzles, they learn basic coding skills and computer science concepts.

With Scratch, we focus on *projects* instead of puzzles. When we introduce kids to Scratch, we encourage them to create their own interactive stories, games, and animations. They start with ideas and turn them into projects that they can share with other people.

Why focus on projects? We see coding as a form of fluency and expression, much like writing. When you learn to write, it's not enough to learn spelling, grammar, and punctuation. It's important to learn to tell stories and communicate your ideas. The same is true for coding. Puzzles might be fine for learning the basic grammar and punctuation of coding, but they won't help you learn to express yourself. Imagine trying to learn to write just by working on crossword puzzles. It could improve your spelling and vocabulary, and it could be fun, but would you become a good writer, able to tell stories and express your ideas fluently? I don't think so. A project-based approach is the best path to fluency, whether for writing or coding.

Even though most people don't grow up to become professional journalists or novelists, it's important for everyone to learn to write. So too with coding—and for similar reasons. Most people won't grow up to become professional programmers or computer scientists, but learning to code fluently is valuable for everyone. Becoming fluent, whether with writing or coding, helps you to *develop your thinking*, *develop your voice*, and *develop your identity*.

DEVELOPING YOUR THINKING

In the process of writing, you learn to organize, refine, and reflect on your ideas. As you become a better writer, you become a better thinker.

As you learn to code, you also become a better thinker. For example, you learn how to break complex problems into simpler parts. You learn how to identify problems and debug them. You learn how to iteratively refine and improve designs over time.

Computer scientist Jeannette Wing has popularized the term *computational thinking* to refer to these types of strategies.

Once you learn these computational-thinking strategies, they can be useful in all types of problem-solving and design activities, not just in coding and computer science. By learning to debug computer programs, you'll be better prepared to figure out what went wrong when a recipe doesn't work out in the kitchen or when you get lost following someone's directions.

Solving puzzles can be helpful in developing some of these computational-thinking skills, but creating your own projects takes you further, helping you develop your voice and develop your identity.

DEVELOPING YOUR VOICE

Both writing and coding are forms of expression, ways to communicate your ideas with others. When you learn to write, for example, you can send a birthday message to a friend, submit an op-ed piece to your local newspaper, or record your personal feelings in a diary.

I see coding as an extension of writing, enabling you to "write" new types of things—interactive stories, games, animations, and simulations. Let me give an example from the Scratch online community. A few years ago, on the day before Mother's Day, I decided to use Scratch to make an interactive Mother's Day card for my mom. Before starting, I checked to see if anyone else had made Mother's Day cards in Scratch. I typed "Mother's Day" in the search box, and I was delighted to see dozens and dozens of projects— many of them created in the previous 24 hours by procrastinators like me!

For example, one of the projects started with the words "HAPPY MOM DAY" drawn on top of a large red heart. Each of the 11 letters was interactive, transforming to a word when touched by the mouse cursor. As I moved the cursor across the screen, touching each letter, a special 11-word Mother's Day message was revealed: "I love you and care for you. Happy Mother's Day mom."

The creator of this project was clearly developing her voice with Scratch—learning to express herself in new ways and integrating coding into the flow of her everyday life. In the future, I believe it will become as natural for young people to express themselves through coding as it is through writing.

(By the way, I didn't end up making a Mother's Day card for my mom. Instead, I sent her links to a dozen Mother's Day projects that I found on the Scratch website. My mom, a lifelong educator, responded with the following message: "Mitch, enjoyed viewing all the kids' Scratch cards so much ... and I love that I'm the mother of a son who helped give kids the tools to celebrate this way!!!!")

DEVELOPING YOUR IDENTITY

When people learn to write, they begin to see themselves differently—and to see their role in society differently. The Brazilian educator-philosopher Paulo Freire led literacy campaigns in poor communities not simply to help people get jobs, but also to help people learn that "they can make and remake themselves" (as he wrote in *Pedagogy of Indignation*).

I see the same potential for coding. In today's society, digital technologies are a symbol of possibility and progress. When children learn to use digital technologies to express themselves and share their ideas through coding, they begin to see themselves in new ways. They begin to see the possibility for contributing actively to society. They begin to see themselves as part of the future.

As we've introduced Scratch to young people, I've been excited by what they've created—and what they've learned in the process. But what excites me most is the way that many Scratchers start to see themselves as creators, developing confidence and pride in their ability to create things and express themselves fluently with new technologies.

TENSIONS AND TRADE-OFFS: KNOWLEDGE

When I heard that Gever Tulley had started a school, I was eager to go see it. Tulley is an engineer who is passionate about providing young people with more opportunities for making things and working on projects. In 2005, just as the Maker Movement was getting started, Tulley created immersive, week-long summer camps where young people worked together in teams to build life-sized projects, such as roller coasters, treehouses, and sailboats. He followed up by creating workshops and after-school programs, all focused on engaging young people in maker-oriented projects.

In 2011, Tulley decided that maker-oriented projects shouldn't just happen outside of school: They should be at the core of school itself. He cofounded a school called *Brightworks*, located in an old warehouse space in the Mission District of San Francisco. Designed for students of ages 5 to 15, the school aimed to combine "the best practices from both early childhood education and hands-on, project-based experiential learning." As described on the school website (sfbrightworks.org): "We use real tools, real materials, and real problems to encourage students' love of learning, curiosity about the world, ability to engage, tenacity to think big, and persistence to do amazing things."

When I visited Brightworks, I saw students working on a wide variety of maker-oriented projects. One team of students was busy constructing an irregularly shaped stage for a school theater production. The students were calculating exactly how much wood they would need for the stage. They explained that the wood was stored on the opposite side of the building, and it was difficult to move the wood, so they wanted to calculate the correct amount before starting to move any of it.

Nearby, another group of students was sitting inside a covered wagon. These students explained that they had constructed the wagon while studying the western migration across the United States, but now they found it convenient to use the wagon as a meeting area on sunny days, because it shielded them from the bright sunlight.

My favorite area was called *Kid City*. Students had been given the opportunity to construct small cubicles for themselves, where they could go to read or write or just for some alone time. At first, the students took the total amount of Kid City space and divided it by the number of students to calculate the size for each private cubicle. But once they constructed the cubicles, they realized that there was no "public space" in Kid City where students could meet or collaborate. So, in an impromptu urban design activity, the students met as a community and debated how much space should be allocated for public use and how to decide on policies for the use of the space.

On my visit to Brightworks, I was accompanied by several executives from a company that sells educational products. As we left the school, I was excited to discuss the power and possibilities of project-based learning, but I quickly discovered that my fellow visitors had a very different impression of the school. "I'm worried that students aren't going to learn the basics," one of them said. "Wouldn't it be better if the school focused on the basics first, and then let students work on projects after that?"

These comments reflect a common concern about project-based learning: It's difficult to predict, ahead of time, exactly what students will learn as they work on projects. When the Brightworks students began building the theater stage, for example, it would have been difficult to know exactly what mathematical concepts they would need to know to finish the job. Wouldn't it be more efficient to develop a list of concepts that are important for students to know, then provide them with problems, examples, and explanations that are specifically designed to teach those concepts?

In fact, that's the way most classrooms are organized. Students are presented with a steady stream of instruction and problem-solving activities, designed to highlight particular concepts. One set of problems teaches students how to multiply fractions. Another teaches them how to calculate the mechanical advantage of a gear train.

On the surface, this approach might seem to make sense. But when students solve sets of disconnected problems, they often end up with disconnected knowledge, without an understanding of why they were learning it or how to apply it in new situations. The project-based approach is much different. As students work on projects, they encounter concepts in a meaningful context, so the knowledge is embedded in a rich web of associations. As a result, students are better able to access and apply the knowledge in new situations.

Even more important, the project-based approach takes a broader view of "knowledge." It recognizes that knowledge is not just a collection of concepts. As students work together on projects, they learn not only webs of concepts, but also sets of strategies—strategies for making things, for solving problems, for communicating ideas. When Brightworks students worked on the Kid City project, for example, they learned strategies for collaborating with others, for understanding different points of view, for making sense of unfamiliar situations.

The project-based approach is particularly well-suited for helping students develop as creative thinkers. As students work on projects, they gain an understanding of the creative process. They learn how to iterate through the Creative Learning Spiral: how to start with an initial idea, build prototypes, share with others, run experiments, and revise their ideas based on feedback and experiences.

Of all the benefits of the project-based approach, perhaps the most important is the way that projects connect to learner interests. As I observed the Brightworks students, it was clear that they cared deeply about the projects they were working on. It was easy to see their sense of pride and dedication as they told stories about their projects and brainstormed about future directions. As we'll discuss in the next chapter, this type of passion (the second of the four P's of creative learning) is an essential ingredient in the creative learning process.

IN THEIR OWN VOICES: JOREN

Joren, also known as JSO in the Scratch community, grew up in Belgium and is now a student at MIT.

Me: How did you get started with Scratch?

Joren: I just turned 12. I enjoyed playing games on the computer, and I was looking for a way to make games myself. I found Scratch, searching on Google, and I started making games. I was really excited that I could share my projects: Here was a community of people that was excited about the same things I was.

My first project was a small game called *Ball Travel*, with a bouncing basketball that travelled to space and back. Somewhere on the Scratch community, I found a way to make the ball bounce so it looked like it had gravity applied to it. I had fun drawing all these levels and creating a story around it. I expected to upload the project to the website so that I could show it to my friends. But before I even got to do that, I got all of these comments and suggestions like "you should add this and this" and "this isn't working too well yet." It was very interactive. That's what kept me coming back.

Me: You joined the Scratch community just as it was starting, in 2007, and you created one of the first "hits" in the community, your virtual LEGO construction kit. How did you come up with the idea for that project?

Joren: My brother and I had been playing with LEGO bricks for a really long time. In fact, it's probably the only toy that we really would use. Around that time, the LEGO company made an application called *LEGO Digital Designer*, which was exciting because I could build things on the screen that I couldn't build in the physical world. I wondered if there was a way to do this for small models in Scratch. I ended up drawing the blocks on a grid, so when you place the blocks on top of one another on the screen, it looks like you're building a 3-D model.

This was one of the first times that I got to explore more math-like things with Scratch, because it's fairly complicated to get the bricks to snap to the grid in the right place. And I needed to learn more about perspective and isometric projection and things like that.

When I shared the project, it became super popular. People used it like a small toy box. Before that, I was happy if anyone looked at my projects, but with this project, it was thousands of people. And they gave me lots of feedback and suggestions.

Me: After a while, in addition to creating your own Scratch projects, you started taking on new roles and leading initiatives to help others in the Scratch community. Can you talk about that?

Joren: I was really drawn to the Scratch community, so I wanted to figure out ways to help the community. At first, I became a moderator in the discussion forums, adding constructive posts to threads, and helping to answer questions from other Scratchers. I also helped create the Scratch wiki, which documents everything that you could imagine about Scratch. It's created by Scratchers, for Scratchers.

My biggest initiative was the Scratch Resources website. Scratch comes with standard libraries of sprites, sounds, and backgrounds, but I thought it would be useful for Scratchers to share their own components with one another. So I created a separate website where Scratchers can upload and share sprites, sounds, and backgrounds. It was useful for the community, and it also gave me an opportunity to learn how to make a community website. I also got to work with other Scratchers, who offered to help with writing some of the code and moderating the site.

Me: How have your experiences with Scratch influenced the way you work on other projects?

Joren: By working on Scratch projects, I've really learned about the process of working on projects. On every Scratch project I worked on, I started with just some vague idea in my head without even being able to formulate what that idea was. Scratch really lets you dive right in and experiment. You create something and then you're like, what are some issues? Sometimes you can fix the problems and you can develop that idea iteratively. At any given point, you can ask yourself, what would I like to add? You think of the next step, and you work on that next step, and then you ask, is this right? If it doesn't work, try to fix it, or ask someone in the community.

As soon as you have a little bit of an idea, you don't really need to theorize about how to formulate it or how to think of a plan to completion, you just have to try something. I try to do that with almost any project: start with something tangible and then keep revising it. You can build a small part and see it running, and then tweak it as you go. Your idea develops as you see what happens.

For mostly everything I've done since 2007, which is a long time for me, a large fraction of my life, this is what I have been doing. When I became interested in building websites, I did it the same way I worked on Scratch projects. And now I learn things at MIT the same way. Whether I'm building a web app or an algorithm or something out of lumber, the iterative approach really works well for me. I try to stick with it wherever I can.

Me: Anything else you've learned from your experiences with Scratch?

Joren: With Scratch, I'm always coming up with my own ideas for projects—and working on problems that I'm interested in. It's exciting to find solutions to problems, but it's even more exciting to find solutions to problems that I've come up with myself. That's a lot more motivational.

Within any kind of assignment or role that I have, it goes so much better if I find something that I'm actually passionate about. It makes a project easier to do, to complete. Whatever the overall goal is, I try to find the most engaging part or the most personally interesting approach to get there.

3

PASSION

BUILDING ON INTERESTS

In December 1989, I got a call from Natalie Rusk, then education coordinator at the Computer Museum in Boston. Natalie wanted to organize some hands-on activities for children and families who would be visiting the museum during the upcoming holiday vacation week, and she asked to borrow some of the LEGO/Logo robotics materials that we were developing at the MIT Media Lab. I saw this as a good opportunity to try out some of our new technologies and activities, so I lent a collection of our LEGO/Logo materials to the museum.

On the second day of vacation week, a group of four children showed up at the museum, speaking to each other in a combination of English and Spanish. One of the boys, age 11, picked up a small, gray LEGO motor. One of the museum mentors showed him how to turn it on. He called out excitedly for his friend to come see: "¡Mira, mira! Look at this!" The children worked together to build a car out of the LEGO materials, then learned how to create a Logo program to control the movements of the car. The children came back to the museum day after day, eager to build more and learn more. After playing with the car for a while, they built and programmed a crane to lift the car. Other children used the LEGO/Logo materials to build and program other machines, including a conveyor belt for a chocolate factory inspired by Willy Wonka.

At the end of the week, we brought the LEGO/Logo materials back to MIT. Everyone was happy with the experience: the children, the museum, our research group at MIT. But the story didn't end there. The next week, the children returned to the museum, saw

Natalie, and asked: "LEGO/Logo?" Natalie explained that the materials were no longer available. The children wandered around the museum trying out the exhibits. But museum exhibits are typically designed for short-term interaction and don't offer opportunities for open-ended design experiences. The children left the museum, disappointed.

A couple weeks later, an administrator at the Computer Museum sent an email to the staff, warning them to be on the lookout for a group of children sneaking into the museum. It turned out that these were the same children who had enthusiastically participated in the LEGO/Logo activities. Now, they were getting into trouble with security.

Natalie and I were motivated to help. Here were children excited to work on creative design projects, but without anywhere to go. Natalie and I checked out community centers in the area to see if any offered after-school programs that might be of interest for these children. At the time, in 1990, community centers were just starting to offer computer-based activities. Some centers offered classes teaching the basics of word processing and spreadsheets; others offered open-access time when youth could play computer games. But none of the centers provided opportunities for youth to develop their own creative projects.

Natalie and I began to envision a new type of learning center that would address the needs and interests of the youth who had snuck into the museum, as well as other youth from local low-income neighborhoods. The result was the Computer Clubhouse, a learning space where young people have access not only to the latest digital technologies, but also to people who can inspire and support them as they develop creative projects.

As we designed the Computer Clubhouse, we paid special attention to the second of the four P's of creative learning: passion. We wanted the Clubhouse to be a place where young people could follow their interests and passions. Some people on the Computer Museum board suggested that we would need to serve pizza every afternoon to attract young people to come. Although we thought it might be nice to provide some food, we didn't think food would be the key to attracting young people. We felt that if we provided young people with opportunities to work on projects they really cared about, they would be eager to come to the Clubhouse, with or without pizza.

And that's what happened when we opened the first Computer Clubhouse in 1993. Young people interested in art, music, video, and animation started coming to the Clubhouse, and they spread the word to their friends. When young people entered the Clubhouse, staff members and adult mentors would ask them about their interests and then help them get started on projects related to those interests. For different youth, the interests took different forms:

• Some youth were excited about particular technologies or media. For example, some wanted to learn how to make videos, others wanted to learn how to mix music, and still others wanted to learn how to make robots.

• Some youth wanted to work on projects related to their hobbies. A Clubhouse member who loved skateboarding created a website with illustrations showing how to execute different skateboarding tricks.

• Some youth were inspired by particular events in their lives. A Clubhouse member whose family had recently immigrated to the

United States on an airplane worked on a series of projects—a video, an animation, and a 3-D model—all featuring airplanes.

• Some youth were inspired by people they cared about. A pair of brothers, whose father had died when they were young, didn't have any photos of their two parents together, so they used Photoshop to mix together individual photos of their mother and father.

Clubhouse members often worked long hours on these projects, coming back to the Clubhouse day after day. At one point, a teacher from a local school came to visit the Clubhouse, and she was shocked to see one of her students working on a 3-D animation project. She said that he was always goofing off in the classroom. She'd never seen him working so hard.

Over the years, we've seen many similar situations with other Clubhouse members. One teenager who showed little interest in reading at school spent hours reading the reference manual for the professional animation software he was using at the Clubhouse. Other youth who seemed disinterested or distracted in school worked nonstop on projects at the Clubhouse.

Compared to most schools, the Clubhouse provides young people with much more freedom of choice. Clubhouse members continually make choices about what to do, how to do it, and whom to work with. Clubhouse staff and mentors help youth gain experience with self-directed learning, helping them recognize, trust, develop, and deepen their own interests and talents.

Much has changed since we started the first Computer Clubhouse more than 20 years ago. Back then, no one had mobile phones and few people had heard of the Internet. Today, technologies are much different, with 3-D printers and the proliferation of social networks, and the initial Clubhouse in Boston has expanded into an international network, with 100 Clubhouses in low-income communities around the world. Amid all this change, the importance of passion has remained a constant, continuing to fuel motivation and learning throughout the Clubhouse Network.

WIDE WALLS

When discussing technologies to support learning and education, Seymour Papert often emphasized the importance of "low floors" and "high ceilings." For a technology to be effective, he said, it should provide easy ways for novices to get started (low floors) but also ways for them to work on increasingly sophisticated projects over time (high ceilings). With the Logo programming language, for example, children can start by drawing simple squares and triangles but gradually create more complex geometric patterns over time.

As my Lifelong Kindergarten group develops new technologies and activities, we follow Seymour's advice and aim for low floors and high ceilings, but we also add another dimension: wide walls. That is, we try to design technologies that support and suggest a wide range of different types of projects. It's not enough to provide a single path from a low floor to a high ceiling; it's important to provide multiple pathways. Why? We want all children to work on projects based on their own personal interests and passions—and because different children have different passions, we need technologies that support many different types of projects, so that all children can work on projects that are personally meaningful to them.

In developing our Scratch programming language, for example, we explicitly designed it so that people can create a wide range of projects—not just games, but also interactive stories, art, music, animations, and simulations. Similarly, as we develop and introduce new robotics technologies, our goal is to enable everyone to create projects based on their own interests—not just traditional robots, but also interactive sculptures and musical instruments. In evaluating the success of our technologies and workshops, one of our main criteria is the diversity of projects that people create. If the projects are all similar to one another, we feel that something has gone wrong; the walls weren't wide enough.

As an example, let me describe a two-week robotics workshop that our MIT research team helped organize for a group of girls, ages 10 to 13, from a Boston-area Computer Clubhouse. We presented the girls at the workshop with a challenge: If you could invent something to improve your everyday life, what would you invent?

The girls had access to many different types of tools and materials at the workshop. There was a table full of craft materials: pom-poms, pipe cleaners, panels of felt, Styrofoam balls, yarn, construction paper, colored markers. Alongside the craft materials were rolls of masking tape, scissors, glue guns, and other tools for cutting and connecting. On another table were large buckets of LEGO bricks, including not only traditional LEGO bricks for building houses and other structures, but also LEGO motors and sensors, and a new generation of programmable bricks small enough to hold in the palm of your hand.

When Tanya saw these materials, she knew right away what she wanted to create: a house for her pet gerbil. She built the house out of LEGO bricks, then used craft materials for decorating and adding furniture. Tanya also wanted her gerbil to have some modern conveniences. She decided to add an automatic door, just like the ones at the supermarket. She connected a motor to the door of the house and placed a light sensor and a programmable brick nearby. Whenever the gerbil came near the door, it cast a shadow on the light sensor, triggering the door to open.

At first, Tanya intended the door just as a convenience for her pet gerbil. Then she realized that she could use the light sensor to collect data about her gerbil. She wondered: What did the gerbil do all night, while she was asleep? Tanya decided to run an experiment. She wrote a program to keep track of every time the gerbil triggered the light sensor (that is, every time the gerbil went in or out of the house). That way, when Tanya woke up in the morning, she could find out what the gerbil had been doing all night. What did she find? There were long stretches of time with no activity at all, when the gerbil was presumably sleeping, but other slices of times with lots of activity. During these bursts of activity, the door to the house repeatedly opened, then shut, opened, then shut, again and again, as the gerbil moved in and out of the house, over and over.

As Tanya experimented with her gerbil house, Maria worked on a very different project. Maria's favorite hobby was rollerblading. She loved racing through the nearby park on her rollerblades, as fast as she could. Maria always wondered how fast she was going as she glided through the park. Maybe the new programmable LEGO bricks could help her figure it out?

One of the adult mentors showed Maria how to attach a tiny magnet to one of the wheels of her rollerblades—and then how to use a small magnetic sensor to detect each time the magnet rotated past. With that, Maria was able to find out the number of times her rollerblade wheels rotated each second. But Maria wanted to know her speed in miles per hour. When she rode in her mother's car, she saw the speedometer read 30 or 40 miles per hour, for example. How did her rollerblading speed compare with the car's speed?

In Maria's school, the teacher had already shown the class how to convert from one unit of measurement to another, but Maria hadn't been paying attention. At the time, it didn't seem to matter much. Now, Maria cared. She really wanted to know how fast she was going on her rollerblades. With some help from a mentor at the workshop, Maria figured out how to do the multiplication and division necessary to convert rotations per second into miles per hour. The resulting speed wasn't quite as fast as she'd hoped, but she was very pleased to have figured it out.

Across the room, Latisha was working on a security system for her diary. Every night, Latisha would write an entry and draw sketches in her diary. Many of the entries were very personal, and she didn't want anyone else to see them, especially not her brother. After seeing a demonstration of the programmable LEGO bricks, Latisha wanted to come up with a way to protect her diary. She attached a touch sensor to the clasp of the diary, and she built a mechanism to press the button on her camera. She wrote a simple if-then rule for the programmable brick: If the touch sensor is pressed (on the clasp of the diary), then turn on the mechanism to press the button on the camera. So if her brother, or anyone else, tried to open the diary when Latisha wasn't around, the camera would take a photo as evidence.

Many factors contributed to the success of the workshop. The girls had easy access to a wide variety of materials—some new, some familiar, some high-tech, some low-tech—to help spark their imaginations. They had enough time to experiment and explore, to persist when they ran into stubborn problems, to reflect and find new directions when things went wrong. They were supported by a team of creative and caring mentors, who asked questions as often as they provided answers. The mentors continually encouraged the girls to try out new ideas and to share their ideas with one another.

Most important, the girls were supported in following their interests. Tanya wasn't building a house for any gerbil, but for her own gerbil. Maria was collecting data related to her favorite hobby. Latisha was protecting her most precious possession. The wide walls of the workshop led to a diversity of projects—and an outpouring of creativity.

HARD FUN

Ben Franklin once wrote: "An investment in knowledge always pays the best interest." I'd suggest a twist on this aphorism: "An investment in interest always pays off with the best knowledge."

When people work on projects that they are interested in, it seems pretty obvious that they'll be more motivated and willing to work longer and harder—but that's not all. Their passion and motivation make them more likely to connect with new ideas and develop new ways of thinking. Their investment in interest pays off with new knowledge.

At first, some youth interests might seem to be trivial or shallow, but with the right support and encouragement, youth can build up networks of knowledge related to their interests. An interest in riding a bicycle, for example, can lead to investigations of gearing, the physics of balancing, the evolution of vehicles over time, or the environmental impact of different modes of transportation.

In visiting Computer Clubhouses, I often meet young people who are disillusioned with school and pay little attention to ideas introduced in the classroom—but when they encounter the same ideas in the context of a Clubhouse project that they care about, they become deeply engaged with them.

On a visit to a Computer Clubhouse in Los Angeles, I met a 13-year-old named Leo who loved playing video games on the computer. At the Clubhouse, working with mentors from Yasmin Kafai's research group, he had learned to use Scratch to create his own games. He proudly showed me one of his Scratch games, and it was clear that he had worked very hard on the project. Building on his interest in playing games, Leo had developed a passion for creating games.

But the day I visited, Leo was frustrated. He felt that his game would be much more interesting to other people if the game could keep score. He wanted the score to go up every time the game's main character killed a monster, but he didn't know how to make it happen. He tried a variety of approaches, but none worked.

I showed Leo a Scratch feature that he hadn't seen before: a variable. Together, Leo and I created a variable called *score*. The Scratch software automatically added a small box on the screen displaying the value of *score*, and it also added a collection of new programming blocks for accessing and modifying the value of *score*. One of the blocks had this instruction: *change score by 1*. When Leo saw this block, he immediately knew what to do. He inserted the new block into his program, wherever he wanted the score to increase. He tried playing his game again, with the newly revised program, and he was excited to see the score increase each time he defeated a monster in the game.

Leo reached out to shake my hand, exclaiming: "Thank you! Thank you! Thank you!" It made me feel good to see Leo so excited. I wondered: How many algebra teachers get thanked by their students for teaching them about variables? That doesn't happen, of course, because most algebra classes introduce variables in ways that don't connect with student interests and passions. Leo's experience at the Clubhouse was different; he cared about variables because he cared about his game.

Such stories are common in the Scratch community: A 12-year-old girl was making an animated story with two characters, and to make the characters meet at a particular point on the screen at the same time, she needed to learn about the relationship between time, speed, and distance. A nine-year-old girl was making an animated book report about *Charlotte's Web* for her third-grade class, and to make the animals appear at different distances, she needed to learn about the art concept of perspective and the math concept of scaling. This learning didn't come easily. The children in these stories worked hard to learn about variables, speed, perspective, and scaling—and they were willing to work hard because they cared about the projects they were working on.

Seymour Papert used the term *hard fun* to describe this type of learning. Too often, teachers and educational publishers try to make lessons easier, believing that children want things to be easy. But that's not the case. Most children are willing to work hard—*eager* to work hard—so long as they're excited about the things they're working on.

When children engage in a hard-fun activity, they also become engaged with the ideas associated with the activity. It's common to hear adults talk favorably about activities that are "so much fun that kids don't even know they're learning." But that shouldn't be the goal. It's valuable for kids to be reflective about their learning, to think explicitly about new ideas and new strategies. After Leo used variables to keep score in his game, he wanted to learn more about variables. What else could variables do? How else could he use them?

The best learning experiences go through alternating phases of immersion and reflection. Developmental psychologist Edith Ackermann described the process in terms of *diving in* and *stepping back*. When people work on projects they're passionate about, they're eager to dive in and immerse themselves. They're willing to work for hours, or longer, and hardly notice that time is passing. They enter a state that psychologist Mihaly Csikszentmihalyi calls *flow*—completely absorbed in the activity.

But it's also important for people to step back and reflect on their experiences. Through reflection, people make connections among ideas, develop a deeper understanding of which strategies are the most productive, and become better prepared to transfer what they've learned to new situations in the future. Immersion without reflection can be satisfying, but not fulfilling.

Passion is the fuel that drives the immersion-reflection cycle. This is true for learners of all ages. When my graduate students at MIT look for topics for their dissertations, I tell them that it's essential for them to find topics they're passionate about. I explain that researching and writing a dissertation is very hard work, with many obstacles and frustrations along the way. There will be times when they will feel like giving up. The only way that they can persist and persevere through all the challenges is if they work on topics that they're truly passionate about.

GAMIFICATION

At the TED conference in 2011, Sal Khan made a presentation called "Let's Use Video to Reinvent Education." In it, he described his work on Khan Academy, an enormously popular website providing short instructional videos that teach lessons in math, science, art, economics, and other disciplines. At the end of the presentation, Microsoft founder Bill Gates joined Khan on stage and asked him a few questions. This part of the exchange caught my attention:

Gates: I've seen some things you're doing in the system that have to do with motivation and feedback—energy points, merit badges. Tell me what you're thinking there?

Khan: Yeah, we've put a bunch of game mechanics in there, where you get these badges. We're going to start having leaderboards by area, and you get points. It's actually been pretty interesting. Just the wording of the badges or how many points you get for doing something, we see on a system-wide basis, tens of thousands of fifth-graders or sixth-graders going one direction or another, depending on what badge you give them.

The audience burst into laughter and applause. They loved the idea that students could be steered this way or that way by offering them points and badges.

This example is hardly unique. Almost everyone, it seems, has bought into the gamification of education. When children play games on the computer, they're clearly motivated by accumulating points and other rewards, so why not apply the same approach to education? If children can get points and rewards in educational activities, as they do in games, won't they be more motivated to learn?

Gamification has become the conventional wisdom. In classrooms, children are rewarded by stickers and gold stars. In educational apps, they're rewarded with points and badges. This approach builds on a long tradition in educational psychology. Researchers like Edward Thorndike and B. F. Skinner, pioneers of a branch of psychology known as *behaviorism*, demonstrated the power of offering rewards to encourage desired behavior. Their theories had a deep influence on management strategies in classrooms and workplaces throughout the 20th century.

But recent research calls into question the long-term value of the behaviorist approach, particularly in creative activities. It's undeniably true that rewards can be used to motivate people to shift their behavior in the short term, but the long-term effects are much different. In his book *Drive: The Surprising Truth About What Motivates Us*, Daniel Pink describes the differences this way: "Rewards can deliver a short-term boost—just as a jolt of caffeine can keep you cranking for a few more hours. But the effect wears off—and, worse, can reduce a person's longer-term motivation to continue the project."

Pink discusses several research studies that demonstrate the limits of using rewards for motivation. In one study, by Edward Deci, university students were asked to solve puzzles by putting blocks together. The students were divided into two groups. The students in one group were paid for each puzzle that they completed, while students in the other group received no pay. Not surprisingly, students in the paid group spent more time on the puzzles than students in the unpaid group. The next day, the students were invited back to solve more puzzles, but this time none of the students received any pay. What happened? The students who had been paid the first time spent less time on the puzzles than the students in the unpaid group. That is, the students who had received pay on the first day became less motivated than the students who had never received any pay at all.

Another study, by Mark Lepper and colleagues, involved kindergarten students rather than university students, and certificates rather than cash, but the results were similar. Some kindergarten students were offered "Good Player" certificates for making drawings on paper, while other students received no certificates. Two weeks later, the children were asked to make more drawings, but no certificates were offered. The students who had received certificates the first time showed less interest and spent less time making drawings the second time.

The effects of rewards are most negative when creative activities are involved. In some studies, researchers asked people to solve problems that required creative thinking, and participants took longer if they were paid for their solutions. The lure of a reward or payment seems to narrow people's focus and restrict their creativity. Similarly, creativity researcher Teresa Amabile analyzed artists' paintings and sculptures, and she found that the artists produced work that was less creative when they were paid for their creations—even when there were no restrictions on what they could create.

If your goal is to train someone to perform a specific task at a specific time, then gamification can be an effective strategy. Turn the task into a game, offering points or other incentives as a reward, and people are likely to learn the task more quickly and efficiently. But if your goal is to help people develop as creative thinkers and lifelong learners, then different strategies are needed. Rather than offering *extrinsic* rewards, it's better to draw upon people's *intrinsic* motivation—that is, their desire to work on problems and projects that they find interesting and satisfying.

That's the approach we've taken with the Scratch online community. Unlike most children's websites, Scratch doesn't offer any explicit points, badges, or levels. Our goal is to keep the focus on the creative activity of making interactive stories, games, and animations. We want young people to come to the Scratch website because they enjoy creating and sharing projects, not because of the lure of prizes and rewards.

Our MIT Scratch Team does select certain projects to feature on the home page. That might be viewed as a type of reward—and, indeed, members of the Scratch community are very excited when their projects are featured. But our intention is to highlight creative projects that can serve as inspiration for the community, not to reward particular community members. If you visit a member's profile page, there's no mention of the number of times that member's projects have been featured. Instead, the main focus of the profile page is on the projects that the member has created and shared. We want Scratch community members to be proud of their portfolio of projects, not the rewards that they've received.

Some Scratch community members try to gamify the site themselves, taking any number that appears on the website and turning it into a competition: Who has the most projects? Who has the most followers? Which project has the most loves? In our design of the Scratch website, we try to discourage this type of competition; we don't want community members spending all their time trying to accumulate the most of this or that. For example, when a community member has created more than 100 projects, their profile page indicates "100+" projects, not the exact number. We'd prefer that members focus on the creativity and diversity of their projects, not who can create the most.

We understand the appeal of extrinsic rewards and gamification, but we also know that intrinsic motivation is the key to long-term engagement and creativity.

PERSONALIZATION

In recent years, it seems as if everyone has become interested in *personalized learning*. The term is embraced by a wide variety of educators, researchers, developers, and policymakers. But there is less consensus than it might seem. When you look closely at what people are saying about personalized learning, it becomes clear that people are using the term in very different ways.

The divergence in how people think about personalized learning became apparent to me a few years ago, when I was asked to give a keynote presentation at a conference organized by a large educational publishing company. I had some reservations about the company because of its role as a leading developer and proponent of standardized tests for schools, but I was intrigued when I saw that personalized learning was a major theme in the conference agenda. Perhaps this was an area where we could find some agree-

ment. On the spectrum between standardization and personalization in education, my preferences certainly lean in the direction of
personalization.

As the conference began, I quickly found that the conference
organizers were thinking about personalization very differently
than I was. The presentations at the conference focused on new
software systems designed to personalize the delivery of instruction
to students. The software periodically asked students questions,
then customized the subsequent instruction based on how students
responded to the questions. If a student gave an incorrect response,
the system provided more instruction on the topic. For example, if
a student made a mistake in converting inches to centimeters, the
system might show an animation or video that illustrated strategies
for converting between different units of measurement.

It's easy to understand the appeal of these personalized systems,
particularly when they're compared with systems that deliver the
same instruction to all students, regardless of what the students
know or how they respond to questions. Who wouldn't want a
personal tutor that continually adapts to your individual needs?
And with continuing advances in the fields of machine learning
and artificial intelligence, the performance of these personalized
tutoring systems is likely to improve in the future.

But I'm skeptical about personalized tutoring systems. One
problem is that these systems tend to work only in subject areas
with highly structured and well-defined knowledge. In these fields,
computers can assess student understanding through multiple-
choice questions and other straightforward assessments. But computers can't assess the creativity of a design, the beauty of a poem,
or the ethics of an argument. If schools rely more on personalized

tutoring systems, will they end up focusing more on domains of knowledge that are easiest to assess in an automated way?

Even more important is the issue of control. Do we really want computerized systems controlling the pace, direction, and content of the learning process? My vision of personalized learning is very different, giving the learner more choice and control over the learning process. I'd like learners to have more control over how they're learning, what they're learning, when they're learning, where they're learning. When learners have more choice and control, they can build on their interests and passions, and learning becomes more personal, more motivating, more meaningful.

Some personalized learning initiatives give learners more control by allowing them to assemble their own "playlists" from collections of "learning modules." Students get to decide when to work on each module and for how long. That's a step in the right direction, but it's still too constraining. In these initiatives, students have control over the order and pacing of activities, but no control over the activities themselves.

As we developed the Scratch programming website, we wanted to make sure that everyone could chart their own personalized paths. We designed the site to support all different types of projects (games, stories, animations) so that everyone could work on projects aligned with their own interests and passions. We included a wide range of tutorials to provide many different pathways for getting started with Scratch. Want to animate your name? There's a tutorial for that. Want to create a pong game? There's a tutorial for that, too. Want to make an interactive birthday card for a friend? Yes, there's a tutorial for that as well.

To help kids personalize their projects, we made it easy for them to import images and sounds from other websites. We also made it easy for them to "put themselves into the project" by using the cameras and microphones on their computers. We developed an easy-to-use paint editor so that kids could draw their own characters and backgrounds for their projects. Some people questioned why we invested so much effort in these media-oriented tools and features. Why not just focus on helping kids learn how to program? Shortly after we launched Scratch, we received this message from a computer scientist (and Scratch parent) who, at first, had been skeptical about our approach:

I have to admit that I initially didn't get why a kids' programming language should be so media-centric, but after seeing my kids interact with Scratch it became much clearer to me. One of the nicest things I saw with Scratch was that it personalized the development experience in new ways by making it easy for my kids to add personalized content and actively participate in the development process. ... They could add THEIR own pictures and THEIR own voices to the Scratch environment which has given them hours of fun and driven them to learn.

The Scratch approach to personalization stands in striking contrast to most learn-to-code websites, which introduce kids to coding through a series of puzzles to solve. Because the puzzles are standardized, the sites can track kids' progress and offer personalized instruction and advice—but they provide kids with little or no opportunity for personal expression. The Scratch approach is diametrically opposed. Because kids can create anything they want with Scratch, it's difficult to automatically provide feedback or guidance—but the payoff comes in connecting with kids' interests and catalyzing their imaginations.

TENSIONS AND TRADE-OFFS: STRUCTURE

People sometimes say that Computer Clubhouses are based on an "unstructured" approach to learning. That annoys me. It's true that we set up Clubhouses to be very different from traditional school classrooms. We didn't want a teacher standing in front of the Clubhouse, delivering lectures, and we didn't want to offer a standardized curriculum, with all Clubhouse members required to work on the same activities at the same time in the same order. But I prefer to think of Clubhouses as having a different structure, rather than no structure.

We show Clubhouse members sample projects to spark their imaginations. That's a form of structure. We organize special events where Clubhouse members exhibit their work. That's also a form of structure. We arrange for adult mentors to help Clubhouse members with their projects. That's a form of structure too.

One of the guiding principles of the Computer Clubhouse approach is that members should be allowed to work on projects they really care about. They should have the freedom to follow their fantasies. At the same time, it's important for us to provide the support and structure that members need to turn their fantasies into realities.

Finding the right balance between freedom and structure is the key to creating a fertile environment for creative learning. That's true in Clubhouses, but also in classrooms, homes, libraries, museums, and all other settings. Too often, people create a dichotomy between freedom and structure, and they put learning environments in one category or the other. The reality is that all learning environments involve some freedom and some structure. The challenge is how to find the right mixture and the right forms of structure.

When new staff members and mentors start working at Computer Clubhouses, they sometimes have trouble understanding the balance between freedom and structure. When they hear that Clubhouses encourage youth to build on their own interests, they assume that adults need to get out of the way and let Clubhouse members do everything themselves. For example, I once heard a mentor propose a workshop to help Clubhouse members learn how to create animated comic books. A Clubhouse staff member initially dismissed the idea, explaining: "We don't do workshops at the Clubhouse. We let Clubhouse members follow their own interests."

That's a misunderstanding of the Clubhouse approach. I would certainly advise against a Clubhouse organizing a mandatory workshop in which all Clubhouse members were required to learn about animated comic books. But as long as members have a choice about whether to participate, I think it's a great idea to offer workshops for Clubhouse members. Such workshops can help Clubhouse members discover what areas they are (or aren't) interested in and help them learn new skills that will be useful in pursuing their interests.

Karen Brennan has done some of the most thoughtful research on these issues, exploring the relationship between *structure* and *agency*. For her PhD dissertation, Karen studied how young people use Scratch in two different contexts: at home (via the online community) and in school classrooms. She noted that people tend to view these two contexts as opposite extremes. The online community is generally viewed as a setting where young people have a lot of agency without much structure; they have the freedom to decide what types of Scratch projects to make and how to make them. On the other hand, school classrooms are usually viewed as places with a lot of structure but not much agency for students.

In her studies, Karen found that there are problems with both too much structure and too little structure. With too much structure, young people can't work on what they want to work on. With too little structure, many aren't able to come up with ideas or follow through on ideas. Karen rejects the idea that structure and agency should be seen in opposition to each other. She argues for the "best of both worlds," proposing learning environments that "employ structure in a way that amplifies learner agency."

Jay Silver has addressed similar issues while developing invention kits for kids (such as Makey Makey, which he co-invented with Eric Rosenbaum). Jay wants his kits to be open-ended so that kids can invent whatever they imagine, but Jay also recognizes that some kids need more structure and support as they are getting started. For many people, there's nothing scarier than a blank page (or blank canvas or blank screen) at the start of a creative project. So Jay aims to create learning environments that are "closed-started" while remaining open-ended—that is, environments that provide more structure or scaffolding at the start of a project, but without restricting learners from pursuing their own interests, ideas, and goals over time.

As we develop future versions of Scratch, we're dealing with similar issues. Although millions of children around the world are now creating games, stories, and animations with Scratch, we know that some children have trouble getting started with Scratch. They look at the Scratch site and feel overwhelmed by all of the options. We need to provide more structure and support to help children get started with Scratch—but, at the same time, we want to make sure that newcomers have the opportunity to follow their interests and passions, since that's at the core of the Scratch experience.

To address this challenge, we are creating a collection of *interest-based microworlds*. Each microworld is a simplified version of Scratch, with a limited set of programming blocks and graphic assets, carefully chosen to support certain types of projects. For example, one microworld is fine-tuned for making hip-hop dance animations. Another microworld is designed for making interactive soccer games. Each microworld is constrained, making it a more comfortable entry point for newcomers, but still open enough so that children can express themselves creatively. And, significantly, children can import their microworld projects into the full Scratch environment, so there is a smooth pathway for children to work on more complex and diverse projects, when they are ready.

Our ultimate goal is providing structure that supports and simplifies the newcomer experience, while still allowing new Scratchers to follow their interests and express themselves creatively.

IN THEIR OWN VOICES: JALEESA

While growing up, Jaleesa was a member of the Computer Clubhouse in Tacoma, Washington. Now, at age 28, she is the coordinator of the Tacoma Clubhouse and also teaches computer science classes at a local high school.

Me: How did you get started at the Computer Clubhouse?

Jaleesa: When I first went to the Computer Clubhouse, I did not want to go. My aunt made me and my younger sister go to the Clubhouse because she didn't like us being at home by ourselves. My mom wasn't home a lot: My parents had just gotten a divorce, and my mom was working full-time and had also gone back to school. So, my aunt took us to the Clubhouse, which was next door to her church.

I started out taking pictures and putting them in a program called Goo where I could distort the faces. I thought it was funny to make funny faces in Goo.

Me: How did you move on to other activities at the Clubhouse?

Jaleesa: Ms. Luversa, the Clubhouse coordinator at the time, really pushed me. She knew that I was capable of doing more than just making funny faces. She would really push me. She wouldn't really give me a choice. She would tell me a project to work on. I'd just be like, "Okay." With Ms. Luversa you couldn't tell her no. One day she came in with computers and she says: "Who wants to help me take apart the computers?" All the boys are like: "Ooh ooh, me me." I just sat there. She's like: "Jaleesa, come on." I was like: "I didn't raise my hand." She's like: "Come on."

I went and we started taking apart the computers and learning the different pieces. Then we took a break, and she said: "You know, if you're really not interested then you can go back up front and work on whatever you want to work on." I stayed. I didn't realize until we were done that I was the only girl that stayed and continued working. After that, Ms. Luversa, she would just push me. "Oh Jaleesa, why don't you work on this? Why don't you learn this? Here's a website that will teach you how to make this. Go look at it. If you have any questions, then ask me." She knew that I was capable of doing more than Goo.

Me: Do you remember particular projects that you were really proud of?

Jaleesa: I really got into making interactive CD-ROMs. The first one that I made was for Black History Month. It was based on a play called "What if There Were No Black People?" and it high-lighted inventions of black people in the United States. I worked with another member. She helped me draw the characters. Then, I put them on the stage and programmed them. It was really exciting because I could show my Mom what I was working on. This was a pivotal point in my life. I became fascinated with learning how I could create anything with technology.

I also started using the Clubhouse to work on things for school. For my English class freshman year, we were studying *Romeo and Juliet*. For our final project, I talked to the teacher and asked if I could make an interactive CD-ROM. He didn't really know what I was talking about, but he's like: "Sure, go ahead." I went to the Clubhouse every day after school and worked on that. I put way more time and effort into it than the other students put into their papers. It was something that I was really proud of.

Me: How did your work at the Clubhouse open up new opportunities for you outside of the Clubhouse?

Jaleesa: Our Clubhouse participated in Microsoft's Student Minority Days. There was an essay contest, and I won a brand new desktop computer. That was really good, because the computer that we had at home was really slow and I didn't like to use it. And Microsoft invited me to apply for a summer internship. I got an offer from the Mobile and Embedded Devices User Assistance Team as a technical writer. I got to do usability studies. That just blew my mind. It just changed the way I thought about everything. I would wake up at 4:30 in the morning every day to get ready and get on the bus. I had to take three buses from Tacoma to Redmond to get to my internship every day. Then, at 5:00 in the afternoon, I'd leave and take three buses back in rush hour traffic, just so I could go to sleep early and do it all over again. That was the summer after my junior year. I also did a second internship with them the summer after my senior year of high school.

Me: Then, you went on to college. How did your Clubhouse experiences influence your college experiences?

Jaleesa: My involvement at the Clubhouse really influenced what I wanted to study in college. Before I started at the Clubhouse, I wanted to do hair. I always wrote that I'm going to do hair. I'm going to own my own beauty salon. After I started going to the Clubhouse, I was like: "You know? Maybe I want to do engineering. Maybe I want to be a computer scientist."

I chose to go to the University of Washington. Initially, I wanted to do computer science. But I took the first courses and I hated it. The lecture was just the teacher up front on a projector writing this code, and we're supposed to be taking notes. And in the quiz sections, we did not touch computers. We had a piece of paper where we had to write everything down. There was no room for trial and error, there was no room for creativity.

Because of my experience with the User Assistance Team at Microsoft, I thought: "Maybe I want to do more about usability. Find out more about how people interact with technology." From doing projects at the Clubhouse, I had seen different ways that youth interacted with technology, so I was very interested in that. So, I shifted my major to human-centered design and engineering. I loved it. It was very interactive. It reminded me of working at the Clubhouse on different projects and working collaboratively with the members and the mentors.

Me: How did you decide what to do after college?

Jaleesa: While I was in undergrad, we had a lot of visits from Google and Apple and Microsoft. But then I talked to one of my old high school teachers about doing AmeriCorps, and I was like, "That's what I want to do. I want to go back to Tacoma and I want to help other students." I ended up working at a community center where I had gone during my senior year in high school. It just made sense to me. Then, after AmeriCorps, I went back to the Computer Clubhouse as the coordinator.

Me: Tell me about your experiences as a Clubhouse coordinator.

Jaleesa: If kids tell me that something is hard, I'm like: "Excuse me, I was at this very Clubhouse where you're at. I sat at that same green table. I went to the same school as you. I know. I lived in this neighborhood. I know."

I'm always trying to find out what Clubhouse members are interested in, so I can help them build on it. There were some girls who were not into computer programing at all. They wanted to come and make pictures. But one of their biggest interests was doing stuff for their community and finding ways for other kids like them to not get in trouble. A lot of their friends had been killed due to gang violence, and they really wanted to find a way to reduce that. That was something that they were really interested in. Then they're like: "Oh, what if we made an app? Oh, I guess we have to learn how to code." And they really took off with it. They went around and interviewed their peers; they put a survey out on Facebook. They really took ownership of it. It was kind of funny because I was like, well, I told you guys to learn how to code. But I didn't really push it on them. I waited for them to be ready, to see a reason for it. And I reminded them that they were capable of doing it.

I want to engage Clubhouse members in STEM [science, technology, engineering, and math] activities, but I want to make sure it's fun and relevant, to make sure it's centered around them. Schools are telling them: "This is STEM, this is what you should be doing." I want to make sure to engage them in what they're doing already in their everyday lives, what's meaningful to them in their everyday lives.

4

PEERS

BEYOND RODIN

A few years ago, the government of Jordan invited me to visit the country. The government had set up a nationwide network of community centers, called Knowledge Stations, where people could get access to computers and learn new job skills. But the initiative wasn't living up to expectations. Not many people were visiting the Knowledge Stations on an ongoing basis.

At the same time, the Computer Clubhouse in Amman, Jordan's capital city, was enjoying great success. The Clubhouse was crowded every afternoon, with young people working on a wide variety of creative projects. Young people kept coming back to the Clubhouse. Some came once a week, others a few times a week, and others every day.

Government officials wondered: Why was the Computer Clubhouse so much more popular than the Knowledge Stations? They asked me to visit and give some advice.

I flew to Jordan and visited several of the Knowledge Stations. The differences between Knowledge Stations and Computer Clubhouses became apparent as soon as I walked through the door. In Knowledge Stations, the computers were lined up on rows of tables, all facing in the same direction, and the rows were packed close together, making it very difficult to walk between the rows. Clearly, the intention was for people to listen to instructions from a teacher at the front of the room, then work individually at their computers. There was no space for people to collaborate—or even to walk around to see what others were working on.

The Computer Clubhouse in Amman had a totally different feel. The tables with computers were arranged in small clusters around the room, making it easy for groups to work together and to check out other people's projects. The chairs all had rolling wheels, so members could easily roll over to another table for a quick conversation or longer collaboration. In the middle of the Clubhouse was a large green table without any computers on it. This table served as a type of village green, where people came together to share ideas, sketch plans, build with LEGO bricks and craft materials—or simply have a snack and catch up. On the walls and shelves around the room were large collections of sample projects, providing newcomers with a sense of the possibilities and with ideas for getting started.

Other Clubhouses around the world have similar setups. Some of the design choices might seem unimportant (or even extravagant), but we've found that the design of the space deeply influences the attitudes and activities of the participants. In particular, the design of the Clubhouse space communicates that this is a place for peer-based learning, where young people learn with and from one another. The design makes it easy for Clubhouse members to work together—and puts them in a mindset for doing so.

Throughout history, thinking and learning have too often been framed as activities done by individuals, on their own. When people think about thinking, they often think of Rodin's famous sculpture *The Thinker*, which shows a lone individual, sitting by himself, in deep contemplation. Of course, some thinking happens that way, but most doesn't. Most of the time, thinking is integrated with doing: We think in the context of interacting with things, playing with things, creating things. And most thinking is done in connection with other people: We share ideas, get reactions from other people, build upon one another's ideas.

Computer Clubhouses aim to go beyond Rodin, shifting from think-it-yourself to make-it-together. This approach is more aligned with the needs of today's society, where almost all jobs require collaborative effort, and the most important social issues require collective action.

At Computer Clubhouses, collaboration comes in many different forms. In some cases, Clubhouse members are simply inspired by what others are working on and don't work together directly. In other cases, Clubhouse members with complementary skills team up to work on a project. For example, a member with video skills and a member with music skills may work together to make a music video, or a member with building skills and a member with programming skills may team up to create a robot.

By working together, Clubhouse members can take on projects that are bigger than any one of them could handle alone. A group of nine fourth-grade girls started coming to a Boston-area Clubhouse after school. After several sessions experimenting with small projects, they decided to work together to create a "city of the future," using some of our robotics technology from MIT. The girls built and programmed elevators, buses, and even a tour guide for the city. They proudly named their creation "Nine Techno Girls City."

Recognizing the growing importance of collaboration skills in the workplace, more schools are starting to add collaborative activities in the classroom—but in many cases, the students are told what to work on and who to work with. In contrast, Clubhouses place a high priority on bringing together the principles of *passion* and *peers*, so that young people not only work together, but also work on projects that they care about. Clubhouse members aren't

assigned to work on teams. Instead, teams come together infor-
mally, coalescing around shared interests and common projects.
Teams are dynamic and flexible, evolving to meet the needs of the
project and the interests of the participants.

At Clubhouses, we try to establish a culture in which members,
as they develop new skills, feel a sense of responsibility to share
their skills with others. When we started the very first Computer
Clubhouse, we were fortunate to have an early member who helped
establish this culture. Mike Lee came to the Clubhouse with a
love of drawing, but without any computer experience. He quickly
learned how to use the computer to create new types of illustrations
that reflected his distinctive artistic style. His projects attracted
attention from other Clubhouse members, who began coming to
him for advice, wanting to learn his techniques and style. Mike was
generous with his time, and soon there was an entire subcommu-
nity of Clubhouse members creating artwork in what they called
the *Mike Lee style*.

When we started the first Computer Clubhouse in 1993, we had
a very local vision of collaboration and peers. We thought mostly
about young people working together, side by side, within the Clubhouse. For the first few years, the Clubhouse didn't have Internet connectivity, so collaboration at a distance would have been
difficult. But as more and more Clubhouses opened around the
world and connectivity became commonplace, new opportunities
for collaboration emerged. Today, there are 100 Clubhouses in 20
countries, connected with one another through an online network
called the Clubhouse Village, so it's now possible for Clubhouse
members to share ideas and collaborate on projects with their peers
around the world. Indeed, when I visited the Clubhouse in Amman,

Jordan, I met a teenage girl who was remixing an anime image that had been created by a Clubhouse member in Chicago.

Our ideas about peers, collaboration, and community today are very different than they were in 1993. Of the four P's of creative learning, peers has probably been the most profoundly affected by new technologies. As we'll explore in the next section, new technologies have dramatically transformed how, when, and where people collaborate—and the roles that peers can play in the learning process.

LEARNING COMMUNITIES

In one of the final chapters of his book *Mindstorms*, Seymour Papert writes about the importance of the social side of learning. He points to Brazilian samba schools as an inspirational model. Samba schools aren't really schools; they're more like social clubs or community centers, where Brazilians come together to create music and dance routines for the annual carnival festival. What struck Seymour was the way that samba schools bring together people of all different ages and all different levels of experience. Children and adults, novices and experts, all work together to create songs and dances that grow out of the traditions and culture of the local community. As people compose, choreograph, practice, and perform at the samba schools, they are constantly learning with and from one another.

Seymour's stories of the Brazilian samba schools have had a big influence on the projects I've worked on over the years. As we set up Computer Clubhouses around the world, we tried to design them in the spirit of samba schools, creating spaces where young people could work together and learn together. As we've developed Scratch, we've tackled a new challenge: How can we bring the ideas and spirit of samba schools to the online world? Or, put another way, how can we take advantage of the new possibilities of the online world while remaining aligned with the core values of successful, physical-world learning environments like samba schools?

Many people think of Scratch as a programming language—and, of course, it is. But those of us working on Scratch see it as much more than that. From the very beginning, our goal was to create a new type of online learning community where young people can create with one another, share with one another, and learn with one another, in the spirit of a samba school. Our top priority was to provide creative learning experiences for young people around the world—and, at the same time, to help teachers, parents, designers, researchers, and others see how online technologies and online communities can support creative learning.

We designed the Scratch programming language and online community as a tightly integrated package, with each supporting the other. After using the programming language to create an interactive game or animation, a Scratcher simply can click the *Share* button to add their project to the online community. Once a project is shared, it's available for anyone in the world to try. In the first 10 years of Scratch, young people shared more than 20 million projects in the online community.

The Scratch online community serves as a source of both inspiration and feedback. By trying out other people's projects, Scratchers learn new coding techniques and get new ideas for their own projects. One 10-year-old Scratcher wanted to make a game with a bouncing ball, but couldn't figure out how to make the ball bounce. "So I looked on the website and found a project with a bouncing ball," she said. "From another project, I learned how to add friction."

When Scratchers share their own projects on the site, they get suggestions and advice from other community members. "With Scratch, I can make projects that I'm excited about, then share the projects with a community of people who share my excitement," explained one Scratcher. "This had been a problem before. I had been trying to program some things, but I couldn't really go anywhere with it. Now I can share my projects and get feedback. That has really driven me to continue."

Within the Scratch community, young people are constantly inventing and exploring new ways to collaborate. Compared with collaborations in traditional school classrooms, Scratch collaborations tend to be more fluid and organic, with people coming together based on shared interests or complementary expertise, much as in a samba school. But unlike a samba school, Scratch brings together people from all over the world, opening possibilities for collaborations that are larger and more diverse.

Here are a few of the ways that young people have been collaborating with one another in the Scratch community.

COMPLEMENTARY PAIRS

A teenager with the Scratch username nikkiperson2 loved to create and share animations in Scratch. One day, while browsing the Scratch website, nikkiperson2 was attracted by a series of projects that focused on a character named Heroine Lisa, created by Scratcher kris0707. nikkiperson2 noticed that the Heroine Lisa projects contained only static images, not animations, so she left a comment on one of the projects, offering to collaborate: "Can I try to make moving sprites of your characters? We could work together to make this animated if you want. But only if you want to. Thanks. (I like these drawings you do.)" kris0707 responded positively to the suggestion, and the two girls collaborated for more than a year on a series of 10 episodes of Heroine Lisa. Through the collaboration, kris0707 learned more about programming with Scratch, and nikkiperson2 learned more about aesthetic expression with Scratch.

EXTENDED TEAMS

Thirteen-year-old Sarah and her ten-year-old brother Mark both love Halloween, so they decided to collaborate on a Scratch project for Halloween. They posted a message about their project on the Scratch forums, and other Scratchers volunteered to help. They decided to create an interactive project in which players navigate a spooky old mansion. Some Scratchers worked on the plot, others on the programming, others on the music, and others on the artwork. In all, more than 20 Scratchers contributed. The final product, called "Night at Dreary Castle," included 59 characters and 393 programming scripts. "One thing I've learned is how to help keep a group of people motivated and working together," said Sarah. "I like Scratch better than blogs or social networking sites like Facebook because we're creating interesting games and projects that are fun to play, watch, and download. I don't like to just talk to other people online, I like to talk about something creative and new."

CHAPTER 4

SUBCOMMUNITIES

The Scratch website includes "studios" that contain collections of projects. Nancy, a middle-school student, decided to create a studio dedicated to anime and manga, her favorite forms of art and animation. She hoped to not only gather inspiring examples of anime projects, but also create a space where anime lovers could meet one another, share ideas, and learn from one another. Before long, hundreds of Scratchers were submitting anime projects for the studio and posting comments in its forum. Many of the projects were tutorials, showing how to draw eyes, bodies, and hair in an anime style and how to animate anime characters. As one contributor wrote: "There are a whole bunch of people on Scratch with AMAZING anime potential, and they just need a little guidance or tips!" Nancy organized three dozen Scratchers to help curate the studio. Within a few months, the studio had more than 250 projects, 1,600 comments, and 1,500 followers.

FEEDBACK STUDIO

Isabella, a 14-year-old, loved getting comments and suggestions on her Scratch projects. She noticed that some projects on the Scratch website weren't getting any comments, and she worried that people might get frustrated and leave the community. Isabella decided to start a Feedback Studio: The idea was to connect Scratchers who wanted to receive feedback on their projects with other Scratchers who enjoyed giving feedback. "People can comment on the projects and share what they liked or ways that they can improve," explained Isabella. "It makes me happy that people are taking advantage of having such an amazing online community." Within days, more than 60 people signed up to curate the studio and give feedback on projects.

CONSULTING SERVICES

One of MyRedNeptune's first Scratch projects was an interactive Christmas card, featuring a collection of animated reindeer playing musical instruments. MyRedNeptune discovered that she especially enjoyed making animated characters (called *sprites* in Scratch), so she created a Scratch project with nothing but sprites. In the project notes, she encouraged other Scratchers to make use of the sprites in their own projects—or to submit requests for other sprites. One Scratcher requested an animation of a cheetah, so MyRedNeptune created a cheetah animation based on a National Geographic video that she found online. For another Scratcher, named Carl, MyRedNeptune created an animated bird with flapping wings. Carl appreciated the sprite, but followed up by asking MyRedNeptune how she had made it, because he wanted to start making animated sprites on his own. In response, MyRedNeptune posted a Scratch project detailing the process that she used to create the bird animation.

Our MIT team explicitly designed the Scratch website to encourage collaboration, so we expected young people to interact and work together on Scratch. Still, we've been continually surprised (and delighted) by the level and variety of collaboration on the Scratch site. Or, at least, I personally have been surprised. Having grown up in the pre-Internet era, I find that I'm not nearly as creative in developing (or anticipating) new forms of collaboration as my MIT students—or the kids in Scratch community. I expect that future generations of kids could become even more creative in the ways they share and collaborate, if we provide them with the right tools, support, and opportunities to do so.

OPENNESS

One of the most important parts of a robotics kit is its programming language—the software that enables you to tell the robot what to do. As my MIT research group collaborated with the LEGO Group on the first Mindstorms robotics kit, we put a lot of time and effort into creating programming software that would be easy for kids to use. At one point, we had a meeting with top LEGO executives to review the plans and strategies for the software. At the meeting, I suggested that the LEGO Group allow other people and organizations to develop alternative programming software for the Mindstorms kit.

The LEGO executives seemed shocked at this suggestion. One of them asked: "What if someone develops software that's better than ours?"

I quickly replied: "That's the whole idea!"

My hope was that openness would lead to more creativity—and better experiences for the kids using Mindstorms. This approach ran counter to the toy industry culture of secrecy and control, so it's not surprising that LEGO executives resisted at first. But, over time, the LEGO Group has moved toward a more open approach in its product development. A few years later, as the company began developing the second generation of Mindstorms, it actively solicited suggestions from the Mindstorms user community, and it published open standards to allow other organizations to produce software and sensors for use with the Mindstorms product.

The LEGO Group even launched a website, called LEGO Ideas, that allowed LEGO fans to propose new LEGO kits, and the company promised to create products based on the most popular submissions. Echoing an idea from Sun Microsystems founder Bill Joy, one LEGO executive explained it like this: "We're proud of our product-development teams. But we also realize that 99.99 percent of the smartest people in the world don't work for the LEGO company."

Openness can enhance creativity in many different ways—not just for organizations like the LEGO Group, but also for individuals. And the benefits of openness are greater now than ever before, thanks to digital technologies. If you're making videos, websites, or other digital creations, you can get ideas and suggestions from people around the world—and also make use of code, artwork, and music created by other people. On the flip side, you can make your digital creations available for others to modify, extend, and integrate into their own projects. This is all possible because digital media, unlike traditional products, can be copied and sent around the world at virtually no cost.

As we developed the Scratch online community, we viewed it as a testbed for openness, hoping to demonstrate how openness and sharing can contribute to children's creativity. In fact, that's why we chose the name *Scratch*; it comes from the "scratching" technique used by hip-hop disc jockeys, who mix music clips together in creative ways. With Scratch, kids can do something similar, mixing code and media clips (graphics, photos, music, sounds) together in creative ways.

We designed the Scratch website so that it's easy for kids to remix (that is, build upon) one another's projects. Each project on the site prominently features a big *See Inside* button. Click the button, and you get access to all the programming scripts and media assets underlying the project. You can drag any of the scripts or assets into your "backpack," so you can use them later in one of your own projects. Or you can click the *Remix* button to get your own copy of the project, which you're free to modify and extend.

Remixing has been enormously popular in the community, right from the beginning. In the first week after the launch of the Scratch website, someone used Scratch to create a simple version of the classic video game Tetris and shared it with the Scratch community. Other members of the community enjoyed playing the game—and many of them had ideas on how to improve it. Within days, there was a proliferation of remixes (and creativity), as other Scratchers extended the game with additional features such as levels, scoreboards, keyboard shortcuts, and lookahead options. If you go to the Scratch website, you can see a visualization of all of the remixes, through multiple generations, somewhat like a family tree. The initial Tetris project has 12 "children"; that is, it was remixed 12 times. One of those children has 560 children of its own ("grandchildren" of the original project). In all, the family tree includes 792 descendants of the original project.

Remixing is one of the primary ways that ideas spread through the Scratch online community. Andres Monroy-Hernandez, who led the development of the first Scratch website, studied this phenomenon in his PhD research at MIT. For example, Andres traced what happened when a Scratcher named Kaydoodle shared a game called *Jumping Monkey*, in which a monkey jumps from one platform to another. Another Scratcher named Mayhem created a simple remix, adding pink slippers to the monkey, to make it easier to detect when the monkey was standing on a platform (based on the color of the slippers). The remix tree continued to grow: The Whiz adapted the pink-slipper technique in his own game, which was then remixed by Deweybears. The remix by Deweybears was a great success, attracting 15,000 views in the Scratch community—compared with only 1,000 views for The Whiz's game, and only 200 views for Kaydoodle's original *Jumping Monkey* project.

The pink-slipper technique continued to spread through the Scratch community, contributing to a proliferation of platform games. Scratchers are constantly looking inside one another's projects, searching for new coding techniques that they can use in their own projects. As one Scratcher told researcher Kyungwon Koh: "The good thing is that because of all of this remixing, every single project out there is a tutorial."

While remixing has sparked creativity in the Scratch community, it's also led to controversy. Some Scratchers aren't happy when their projects are remixed, complaining that their work has been "stolen" by someone else. One fifth-grader even gave a TEDx talk on this topic. Here's how she started her presentation: "I had just finished my best animation yet, and then I saw this," showing a remixed version of her project. "All my hard work, my best animation, ruined ... I got mad, and to be honest, I still am." She's not the only one. When Scratchers write to us with suggestions on how to improve Scratch, one of the most common suggestions is that Scratchers should be able to control whether or not their projects can be remixed.

In general, we try to be responsive to suggestions from the Scratch community, but not in this case. The ability to remix is tightly aligned with our core values of openness and creativity. In setting up the Scratch website, we decided that all projects should be covered by what's called a Creative Commons Attribution license, which means that you're allowed to modify and remix any project on the Scratch website, so long as you give appropriate credit.

It's not surprising that many Scratchers are skeptical about remixing. At school, students are taught to do their own work. Building on the work of others is typically seen as cheating. With Scratch, we're trying to shift the way that kids think about these issues. Our goal is to create a culture in which Scratchers feel proud, not upset, when their projects are adapted and remixed by others. On the website's forums, we discuss the value of sharing and openness. We've continually added new features to the website in an effort to shift the ways Scratchers think about remixing. For example, the Scratch homepage now prominently features a row of the Top Remixed projects, to emphasize that it's an honor for your project to be remixed.

At a recent conference, I was approached by Krishna Rajagopal, a physics professor at MIT. He told me that his sons had become actively involved with Scratch, and he wanted to thank me for creating Scratch. That's always nice to hear. I expected that he would go on to describe the coding skills and computational ideas that his sons were learning. But that's not what interested Krishna the most. Rather, he was excited that his sons were participating in an open knowledge-building community. "It's like the scientific community," he explained. "Kids are constantly sharing ideas and building on one another's work. They're learning how the scientific community works."

CULTURE OF CARING

In the opening chapter of their book *A New Culture of Learning*, Douglas Thomas and John Seely Brown tell the story of a nine-year-old boy named Sam, who enjoyed using Scratch to create animations and games. In one of his games, Sam used a photo of the Grand Canyon as a backdrop and programmed a piece of paper to drift across the landscape, as if blown by the wind. To score points, the player needed to maneuver through the Grand Canyon to catch up with the wind-blown paper.

Sam's favorite part of Scratch was the online community. Sam spent hours examining, remixing, and commenting on other people's projects. The authors of *A New Culture of Learning* asked Sam what it meant to be a good member of the Scratch community: "We were surprised by his answer. It had nothing to do with building games or posting animations. Instead, Sam told us that the single most important thing was to 'not be mean' in your comments and to make sure that you commented on something good when you came across it, as well. [Scratch] does not just teach programming; it cultivates citizenship."

I was happy to read this description. As our team at the MIT Media Lab developed the Scratch online community, one of our top priorities was to foster a culture of caring—an environment where community members respect one another, support one another, and care about one another.

That's not the case in many online communities. It's all too common to find rude, crude, and disrespectful comments on online message boards and discussion forums. People often interact more harshly online than they ever would in face-to-face interactions. When organizations create online communities for kids, they often try to avoid these problems by sharply restricting the ways that kids can interact with one another. For example, if kids want to add images to projects, they're forced to select from predetermined collections of images, rather than creating or importing their own. If kids want to make comments or send messages, they're forced to select from predetermined lists of comments, rather than writing their own.

In developing the Scratch online community, we didn't want to impose those types of restrictions. We wanted to provide members of the Scratch community with the freedom to express themselves creatively and share their ideas with one another. At the same time, we definitely didn't want to tolerate the rudeness and crudeness that is so common in open online interactions. Indeed, we felt that mean-spirited and disrespectful behavior on the site would undermine precisely the types of activities and values we were hoping to promote.

That's why we've worked hard to create a culture of caring in the Scratch online community. It's not just that we value caring, respectful behavior in and of itself (although we do). Even more, we value what it enables. When people feel they're surrounded by caring, respectful peers, they're more likely to try new things and take the risks that are an essential part of the creative process. When people worry that others in the community might ridicule them for their comments or projects, they're less likely to share their evolving ideas and creations.

To encourage a culture of caring in the Scratch community, we established a set of Community Guidelines, which are linked from the bottom of every page on the website. The guidelines include the following:

• *Be respectful.* When sharing projects or posting comments, remember that people of many different ages and backgrounds will see what you've shared.

- *Be constructive.* When commenting on others' projects, say something you like about it and offer suggestions.
- *Be honest.* Don't try to impersonate other Scratchers, spread rumors, or otherwise try to trick the community.
- *Help keep the site friendly.* If you think a project or comment is mean, insulting, too violent, or otherwise inappropriate, click Report to let us know about it.

Of course, just creating and displaying a list of guidelines isn't enough. Members of our MIT Scratch Team are constantly modeling the community guidelines through our own comments and behavior on the website, and we have a team of moderators constantly monitoring the site. When community members violate the guidelines, the moderators give feedback, warnings, and advice—and sanctions if someone has multiple violations. During the summers, we run online camps in which kids not only learn new programming skills but also learn how to give constructive feedback to one another.

To sustain a culture of caring, community members themselves must ultimately take the lead in supporting, encouraging, and reinforcing the community values. For example, it was kids in the Scratch community (not our MIT team) who organized a Welcoming Committee, mobilizing hundreds of experienced Scratchers to provide advice and encouragement to new community members. Champika Fernando wrote an entire master's thesis about "Scratchers helping Scratchers." In it, she documented the many ways that Scratch community members support one another, and she then proposed new strategies and structures for encouraging these types of interactions in the community.

Scratch community members use not only text comments but also animated Scratch projects as a medium for expressing empathy, encouragement, and compassion. For example, one Scratcher created a project titled *Cheer Up Sparkygirl* to express support for a friend who was feeling sad and lonely. Another Scratcher named SmileyFace72 created a series of projects with titles like *Friends are Friends, Don't Stress,* and *You Are Never Too Old.* One of SmileyFace72's projects received more than 15,000 views, 2,000 loves, and 1,900 comments. The outpouring of support for SmileyFace72's projects highlights the reinforcing nature of empathy in the Scratch community; empathetic projects tend to draw an empathetic response.

This culture of caring has made Scratch community members feel comfortable exploring sensitive and personal issues in their projects. In recent years, there has been a surge of Scratch projects related to sexual orientation and gender identity, with Scratchers sharing information, beliefs, and personal stories—and celebrating diversity and inclusion. In general, the community response to these projects has been caring and supportive, which in turn has encouraged other Scratchers to share similar types of projects.

But there have also been challenges. For example, some Scratchers with strong religious beliefs have posted comments and projects arguing that homosexuality is wrong. Our Scratch Team moderators remove these types of comments and projects, with the following explanation: "It's important that Scratch is a welcoming place for people of all ages, races, ethnicities, religions, sexual orientations, and gender identities. Scratchers are free to express their religious beliefs, opinions, and philosophies—so long as they don't make other Scratchers feel unwelcome." This perspective has been echoed by many Scratchers themselves. In a project titled *Empathy*, one Scratcher wrote: "We live in a world where people have many different opinions and beliefs. We all want to express ourselves—express our opinions, our beliefs, our personality. But when doing so, it's important to understand how someone else might feel about what you say. There's a difference between sharing your beliefs and being respectful because of what you believe."

Fostering a culture of caring is, of course, just as important in physical world communities as in online communities. When we started the first Computer Clubhouse after-school center, we developed a set of guiding principles, including *Support learning through design experiences* and *Cultivate an emergent community of learners*. But perhaps our most important guiding principle was *Create an environment of respect and trust*. We recognized that none of the other principles could be put into practice without this one. Only in an environment of respect and trust, in a culture of caring, would Clubhouse youth feel safe enough and comfortable enough to experiment with new ideas and collaborate with new people.

As the network of Clubhouses has grown to 100 sites around the world (led by Clubhouse Network Director Gail Breslow), we've seen the value of this guiding principle. We've found that Clubhouses that establish an environment of respect and trust are best able to build a community of members who come back consistently, work collaboratively, and express themselves creatively. I remember visiting a Clubhouse in Costa Rica that was just finishing its first year. I asked the coordinator about the lessons he'd learned during that first year. "When I started, I was focused on helping members learn about the technology," he said. "But by the end of the year, I realized that the Clubhouse is like a family. What's most important is that everyone cares about one another, and helps one another. If that happens, everything else will work out."

TEACHING

In 1997, the Computer Clubhouse won the Peter F. Drucker Award for Nonprofit Innovation. As part of the award, the Drucker Institute produced a video featuring interviews with Clubhouse members. Francisco, one of the earliest Clubhouse members, discussed how much he had learned from his interactions with Lorraine Magrath, a Clubhouse mentor. "Working with mentors is very exciting. They're fun, and they're funny too," said Francisco. "They're not like teachers. Teachers just tell you: Do this, do that. With a mentor, you feel more friendly, more relaxed to talk to." Francisco went on to describe how Lorraine had provided guidance and advice as he created projects with software packages like Photoshop and Premiere.

Every time I watch the video, I smile when Francisco describes the important role that Lorraine played in his learning experiences at the Computer Clubhouse. It's exactly what we had hoped for when we started the first Clubhouse. From the beginning, we saw mentoring as a core component of the Clubhouse approach. On the other hand, I cringe every time I hear Francisco say "Teachers just tell you: Do this, do that." It makes me sad to consider what Francisco's interactions with teachers must have been like, to lead him to think about teachers in this way.

Unfortunately, Francisco's views on teachers and teaching are shared by many others. As students go through school, they often experience teaching as the delivery of instruction ("Do this, do that") and the delivery of information ("Here's what you need to know"). As evidenced by Francisco's remarks, this approach to teaching can be de-motivating for many learners. What's more, this approach steers learners away from the types of creative experimentation that is so important in today's world, leading them to imitate rather than innovate. Psychologist Alison Gopnik discussed this problem in an op-ed article in the New York Times in 2016. "When children think they are being taught, they are much more likely to simply reproduce what the adult does, instead of creating something new," Gopnik wrote. "The children seem to work out, quite rationally, that if a teacher shows them one particular way to do something, that must be the right technique, and there's no point in trying something new."

Clearly, there are big problems with the traditional teaching strategy of delivering instruction and information. So what's the alternative? Some people go to the opposite extreme, arguing that children are naturally curious and can figure everything out on their own. They often refer to Jean Piaget's famous quote: "When you teach a child something, you take away forever his chance of discovering it for himself." Some people interpret this to mean that the best way to help children learn is simply to stay out of their way.

Too often, teaching strategies are viewed as a dichotomy. *Option 1:* Deliver instruction and information. *Option 2:* Leave children alone and let them learn. When new mentors start working at Computer Clubhouses, we often see examples of these two extremes. Some new mentors try to act like traditional classroom teachers, delivering instruction to Clubhouse members. Others stand back and get involved only if Clubhouse members specifically ask for help.

Indeed, one of the biggest challenges in setting up a new Computer Clubhouse is helping the staff and mentors develop a more nuanced understanding of the teaching process, steering them away from the two extremes. As I see it, good teaching involves playing a variety of different roles, all in the service of helping others learn. Good teachers and good mentors move fluidly among the roles of catalyst, consultant, connector, and collaborator:

• *Catalyst:* In chemistry, catalysts provide the "spark" that accelerates a chemical reaction. Similarly, teachers and mentors can provide the spark that accelerates the learning process. When learners get stuck in the early stages of a project, a teacher might show sample projects to spark their imaginations and provide a sense of what's possible. Often, the best way for a teacher to provide a spark is to ask questions. At Clubhouses, we encourage mentors to ask questions, such as "How did you come up with that idea?", "Why do you think that happened?", "If you could change one part of your project, what would you change?", or "What was most surprising to you?" By asking the right types of questions, a teacher or mentor can catalyze exploration and reflection, but the learner remains that active agent, in charge of the activity.

• *Consultant:* There's an old saying that a teacher should be a "guide on the side," not a "sage on the stage." Clubhouse mentors can serve as guides or consultants in several different ways. Some mentors might be viewed as technical consultants, offering tips and advice on the use of new technologies. Other mentors serve as creative consultants, helping Clubhouse members iteratively develop and refine their ideas into projects. Sometimes, mentors provide emotional support, helping members to overcome their doubts and cope with their frustrations. In all cases, the goal is not to "deliver instruction" or "provide answers," but to understand what Clubhouse members are trying to do and figure out the best way to support them.

• *Connector:* Teachers and mentors can't single-handedly provide learners with all the support they need. So an important part of their job is to connect learners with other people who they might work with, learn with, and learn from. As a mentor and later coordinator at the flagship Computer Clubhouse in Boston, Jackie Gonzalez was constantly looking to connect Clubhouse members with one another. "A good day for me is just getting young people to help other young people," she said. "If I see a teen who needs help with Photoshop for a project they're working on, I'll look for another Clubhouse member who can help. My goal is to create a community of shared learning."

• *Collaborator:* Clubhouse mentors don't simply provide support and advice to Clubhouse youth. We encourage mentors to work on their own projects and invite youth to join in. For example, two graduate students from a Boston-area university decided to start a new robotics project at a local Computer Clubhouse. For several days, they worked on their own; none of the youth seemed particularly interested. But as the project began to take shape, a few youth took notice. One decided to build a new structure to fit on top of the robot; another saw the project as an opportunity to learn about programming. After a month, a small team of people was working on several robots. Some youth were integrally involved, working on the project every day. Others chipped in from time to time, moving in and out of the project team. The process allowed different youth to contribute to different degrees and at different times.

At Computer Clubhouses, we're always trying to blur the boundaries between teaching and learning. As teenagers spend more time at a Clubhouse and become more embedded in the Clubhouse culture, we encourage them to take on mentoring responsibilities: sharing their experience and expertise with other members, and introducing newcomers to the ideas, activities, and technologies of the Clubhouse. Our hope is that, over time, Clubhouse members will learn to serve as catalysts, consultants, connectors, and collaborators within the community, helping others learn while also continuing their own learning.

At the same time, we encourage adult mentors to see themselves as lifelong learners—not just for their own sake, but as a model for youth. One of our top priorities at the Clubhouse is to help youth develop as great learners. By observing adult mentors in the process of learning, youth can learn strategies that they can apply to their own learning. Too often, adults try to hide what they don't know. At Clubhouses, we try to create an environment where mentors feel comfortable acknowledging what they don't know, and talking openly about their strategies for learning new things. Just as aspiring carpenters learn through apprenticeship with master carpenters, we want Clubhouse youth to have the opportunity to observe and work with master learners.

Of course, the framework of catalysts, consultants, connectors, and collaborators isn't specific to Computer Clubhouses. The same strategies can be applied in all learning environments, from school classrooms to online communities. Some people expect that new technologies will reduce the need for teachers, as learners gain access to computerized tutors that can provide advice whenever it's needed. I expect the opposite: New technologies will greatly expand the number of teachers—if we think about teaching in the right way. In an online community like Scratch, everyone can become a teacher, serving as a catalyst, consultant, connector, and collaborator for others in the community.

TENSIONS AND TRADE-OFFS: EXPERTISE

In 1998, the MIT Media Lab organized an event called the Junior Summit. It was the same year that Google was founded, and long before Facebook or Twitter. Most people were just becoming aware of the Internet. The Junior Summit was one of the first large-scale experiments to explore what might happen when large numbers of young people from around the world connect with one another online. In the first phase of the project, 3,000 young people (ages 10 to 16) from 130 countries interacted in online forums, discussing how they could use new technologies to address some of the biggest challenges facing the world. In the second phase, the online participants selected 100 youth representatives to come to MIT for a week of face-to-face collaboration. By the end, the youth had developed plans for several initiatives: an online global newspaper for children, an online KidzBank to support microfunding of social-entrepreneurial projects developed by children, and a new "cyber country" (called *Nation1*) that would offer citizenship to anyone under the age of 19.

When the Junior Summit was in its planning stages, we discussed it at a Media Lab faculty meeting. Justine Cassell, then a professor at the Media Lab and lead organizer of the Junior

Summit, explained the plans for connecting young people from around the world. At the time, it was a bold and innovative idea, and most Media Lab faculty were excited about the possibilities. But then Marvin Minsky, one of the founding fathers of the field of artificial intelligence, spoke up: "This is the worst idea I've ever heard," he said. "Kids have all sorts of bad ideas and misconceptions. If you connect lots of kids together, they'll reinforce one another's bad ideas."

I didn't agree with Marvin's assessment, but his comments provoked me to think. We've certainly seen how the Internet can serve as an echo chamber, with misinformation reverberating throughout a community, continually reinforced by others who have similar misconceptions or misunderstandings. And it's true that children can't learn everything on their own, even if they're working together, supported by their peers. A group of children, even very bright and curious children, won't reinvent calculus on their own—or even recognize the need for calculus.

Peers aren't always enough. Sometimes, there's a need for "experts" in the learning process. But in what situations is outside expertise needed? What can be learned without outside expertise, and what can't? And what's the best way and the best time to bring outside expertise into the learning process?

We grappled with these questions throughout the Junior Summit. The same questions arose in another project that started a year after the summit. In 1999, an Indian physicist named Sugata Mitra installed a kiosk with an Internet-connected computer in the impoverished Kalkaji neighborhood in Delhi. He didn't include any instructions and he didn't run any workshops for residents of the neighborhood. He was interested in what he called *minimally invasive education*. He wanted to see what would happen if he simply provided a computer and Internet connection, without any instruction or supervision. The project became known as the Hole-in-the-Wall experiment, because the neighborhood residents had access to the computer through a hole in a wall.

The Hole-in-the-Wall computer quickly became popular with children throughout the neighborhood. None had ever used a computer before, but they quickly figured out how to navigate the file system and Internet websites. They spent hours experimenting and exploring, finding games and other activities. They organized schedules to coordinate who could use the computer at which times. They shared their knowledge with one another, passing along tips and tricks for using popular programs and finding useful information.

The Hole-in-the-Wall experiment attracted interest from around the world. It became an iconic symbol of what children from all backgrounds can do with new technologies. The World Bank provided funding to install similar kiosks in 80 locations around India, and other organizations created their own variants of the project in other parts of the world. The Hole-in-the-Wall project served as inspiration for many people in many ways. The Oscar-winning movie *Slumdog Millionaire* was inspired, in part, by stories from the Hole-in-the-Wall sites.

I visited the original Hole-in-the-Wall site in Delhi not long after it opened. It was clear that children in the neighborhood were actively engaged in learning and sharing ideas. I was impressed with the project—but I wasn't surprised by it. I've seen many children, in many locations around the world, figure out how to navigate computer applications on their own or with their friends.

For me, what was surprising was how people around the world reacted to the Hole-in-the-Wall experiment. Most people tend to underestimate children's abilities, not recognizing how much children can accomplish and learn through their natural inclination to explore, experiment, and collaborate. I was glad that the Hole-in-the-Wall project opened people's eyes to the extraordinary potential of all children.

On the other hand, I was worried that some people over-interpreted the Hole-in-the-Wall results. Some people took the Hole-in-the-Wall experiment as evidence that children could learn almost anything on their own or with their peers, if only they had access to computers and the Internet. As much as I appreciated what the Hole-in-the-Wall children were able to accomplish, I was equally aware of what they weren't able to do. Although the children quickly learned how to navigate to popular websites and use basic applications, few of them were able to use the Hole-in-the-Wall computer for designing, creating, and expressing themselves. They learned to find and play games on the computer, but they didn't create their own games. They learned to browse the web, but they didn't create their own websites.

Sugata Mitra, the creator of the Hole-in-the-Wall project, recognized that non-peer support is needed for some types of learning experiences. In Sugata's more recent projects, he has continued to provide children with new ways of collaborating with their peers, in what he calls *self-organizing learning environments*—but Sugata now puts greater emphasis on adults as mentors and facilitators. In one online-learning initiative, he set up a network of retired school-teachers, who offered mentorship and encouragement to groups of students as they worked together on online projects.

Peers, as the third P in the creative-learning framework, clearly play an important role in the learning process. But when are peers enough? When should educators and parents encourage children to figure things out on their own or with their peers? When do learners need outside expertise and guidance? We live in an era when all the world's information is available at a child's fingertips, but that doesn't mean children will necessarily know what information to look for or how to make sense of the information they find. We need to provide children with appropriate mentorship and guidance—and help them learn, over time, how to find people and organizations that can provide the support and expertise they need.

IN THEIR OWN VOICES: NATALIE

Natalie, also known as ipzy in the Scratch online community, is a first-year college student in California.

Me: How did you get started with Scratch?

Natalie: I've always been interested in art. I've been drawing basically since preschool, when I learned how to hold a crayon. When I was 11, a friend told me that I could use Scratch to bring my art to life. That was exciting for me.

I remember the very, very first project I ever made was a virtual puppy game. I drew a little dog, and it was very crudely drawn. I programmed it so that you could press certain buttons to do actions. When you press E, your dog will eat. When you press B, he'll bark. Things like that. Very, very simple. I slowly built up my skills by exploring the program and other people's programs. I was able to start with something that I was very comfortable with—drawing—and gradually add more and more programming.

I'm an artist, but I learned that I have an interest in programming, too. I never thought I could do the coding part. I thought I could do art, but I'd have to wait until I'm a grown up and hire someone to code it for me. When I tried Scratch, it was like, hey, I can actually do this myself.

Me: I saw that one of your early projects was based on the *Warriors* books.

Natalie: I was a huge fan when I was in middle school. I think there's thirtysome books, and I had all of them. So, I was really excited when I went on Scratch and saw a bunch of other kids were interested in warrior cats, too. I didn't have any friends in real life who read those books, so it was really exciting for me to meet other kids who loved the warrior cats.

Me: How else do you interact with the Scratch community?

Natalie: Instead of me just sitting alone doing a drawing, I can collaborate with other people and make something interactive that other people can use. They can play with it and make it their own. People can offer help and advice.

I made a project called *Lemonade Time*, where you can walk around and collect items, like lemons and sugar, that you use to create lemonade. That project got featured on the Scratch website, which really encouraged me. I got a lot of comments from people: "Oh cool game!" "Oh I love your art!" People started remixing it and creating new things from it, which showed me that other people were learning from what I made. I thought that was just the coolest thing and wanted to keep making more.

I would get comments all the time from people asking if they could use my art. Obviously, they could just go inside my projects and get it, but I decided to make it easier for them. I made a Scratch project that put my art in one place, sorted out, like, here's animals, here's some backdrops. It made it easy for people to come and find my artwork.

A few years ago, I would get kind of bummed out when people would use my Scratch art, because I was like, "I worked so hard on this, and then they're just taking it." But now, I actually get really happy when people remix my projects and change things. I really like seeing what people do with remixing my projects.

Me: I know you've also created tutorials for the community.

Natalie: A lot of times, people will comment on my page, saying, "I wish I could draw like that" or "I'll never be that good." I want to show them that it's not just magically coming up with a piece of art. There's a process to it, and it's a really easy process once you learn how to do it. It's kind of showing that there's steps to it, and you can improve. It's not just that I'm magically born with artistic talents. It's something that you can do, too.

My work on Scratch got me interested in teaching art. I'm in college now and I'm interested in getting a teaching credential, because I'd love to teach art to kids and get them interested in all aspects of art. Whether it be drawing or coding, because that's an art in itself.

Me: I saw that you're now collaborating with other community members on a multi-animator project. Can you tell me more about that?

Natalie: I got really into animation recently, and I made a little animated music video, which took me weeks to make. I really want to make another one of these, Disney themed, but I don't want it to take forever. So, I was like, hey, I can just do a collaboration and then we can all make it, and then it'll go by a lot faster. I decided to organize a multi-animator project, with a Disney song and animated Disney characters. I had never hosted a multi-animator project on Scratch, so I looked up a Scratch tutorial on how to do it. That was really helpful to me: It showed how to divide up the audio and stuff.

So, I had people sign up for their parts, and people are animating them. In a couple weeks, I'm going to put the whole thing together and post it. Right now, it's 16 people, plus me. With the one that I made by myself, that one took me a few weeks of nonstop work. That was an intense experience, and also I was just working by myself, so that was not as much fun. With the multi-animator project, it's a lot less work, and it's a lot more fun, because then I get to see what everyone else is making, and I get really excited whenever someone posts their finished part. I'm just so excited for it to be done.

Me: Has your work in the Scratch community influenced the way you think about collaborations in other parts of your life?

Natalie: My high school was all project based, which was a really good fit for me. All of the classes were around 25 students, and you had the same kids in your class through the entire year, so it was like a little family. The teachers were really close with their students because they had them all day for a whole year, and I really appreciated that. Also, we were always working on group projects. With some projects, you could choose your partners, but with most of them it was randomly assigned, so you had to learn to work with people who were different than you. That was a good experience for me. It helped me learn how to work as part of a creative team, like on Scratch. Everything is different now in college. Every class is a different set of people, so you don't really get to know anyone. And pretty much all of the work is solo. So, I'm glad that I have Scratch for my collaborations.

5

PLAY

PLAYFULNESS

In the 1990s, an annual conference called *Doors of Perception* brought together researchers, designers, and technologists from around the world to discuss the implications of the Internet and other emerging technologies. The conference was held in Amsterdam, and it focused on a different theme each year. In 1998, the theme of the year was "Play," and I was invited to make a presentation about my work.

The conference showcased the latest computer games, electronic toys, and virtual reality systems. Conference participants flocked around an interactive demonstration featuring the popular video game character Lara Croft. In my presentation, I talked about my group's work on LEGO Mindstorms and other electronic construction kits, and I argued that "playing" with technology should involve not just interacting with it, but designing, creating, experimenting, and exploring with it.

After my presentation, I decided to take a break from the conference and walked to the Anne Frank House, where teenager Anne Frank and her family had hidden in a secluded annex of the house to escape the Nazi persecution of Jews during World War II. I felt uneasy about skipping part of the conference. The following day, I was scheduled to participate in a wrap-up session to reflect on what we had learned throughout the conference, so I felt like I was shirking my responsibility by missing part of the conference. But I really wanted to visit the Anne Frank House. During my childhood, growing up in a Jewish household, I had heard many stories about the persecution of Jews during World War II, and I wanted to learn more and to feel a more direct connection.

My visit to the Anne Frank House was full of surprises. It turned out that Anne Frank and I have the same birthday (June 12), and she was born the same year as my mother (1929). But by far the biggest surprise was that my trip to the Anne Frank House was totally relevant to the play theme of the conference. It turned out that I wasn't shirking my responsibility at all; indeed, I felt that I learned more about the true nature of play at the Anne Frank House than at the conference.

People generally don't associate Anne Frank with play. Anne was in hiding for two years, from mid-1942 to mid-1944, from age 13 to age 15, with no chance to go outside and play. In her diary, Anne describes herself as "desperately unhappy," and writes that "we've almost forgotten how to laugh." She was aware that many of her friends and relatives might be imprisoned in concentration camps or no longer alive. Anne took medication "to fight the anxiety and depression" but reported "it doesn't stop me from being even more miserable the next day."

Despite all of this, Anne's playful spirit shines through in her diary. At one point, Anne wanted to try ballet but didn't have appropriate shoes, so she redesigned her gym shoes into ballet slippers. For St. Nicholas Day, she wrote a pun-filled poem and hid presents for other family members in their shoes. Anne's mind was alive with imagination. "I don't think building sand castles in the air is such a terrible thing to do," she wrote in her diary.

Although living in a cramped space and beset with sadness and scarcity, Anne was constantly experimenting, taking risks, trying new things, testing the boundaries. In my view, those are the essential ingredients of play. Play doesn't require open spaces or expensive toys; it requires a combination of curiosity, imagination, and experimentation.

At times, Anne Frank lost her ability to laugh, but she never lost her playful spirit. Throughout her diary, Anne contrasts herself with her older sister Margot. "Margot is such a goody-goody, perfection itself, but I seem to have enough mischief in me for the two of us put together," wrote Anne. "I've always been the clown and mischief maker of the family."

I sometimes refer to *play* as the most misunderstood of the four P's of creative learning. People often associate play with laughter, fun, and having a good time. It's easy to understand why: Play often involves all those things. But that description misses what's most important about play—and why play is so important to creativity. Creativity doesn't come from laughter and fun: It comes from experimenting, taking risks, and testing the boundaries. Or, in Anne Frank's words, being a mischief maker.

Throughout history, philosophers and psychologists have recognized the value and importance of play:

You can learn more about a person in an hour of play than in a year of conversation.
—Plato

We don't stop playing because we grow old; we grow old because we stop playing.
—George Bernard Shaw

In play, it is as though the child were trying to jump above the head of his normal behavior.
—Lev Vygotsky

Play is the work of the child.
—Jean Piaget

Through play, more than any other activity, children achieve mastery of the external world.
—Bruno Bettelheim

Toys and games are the preludes to serious ideas.
—Charles Eames

I've been particularly inspired by John Dewey, who shifted the focus from play (the activity) to playfulness (the attitude). He explained: "Playfulness is a more important consideration than play. The former is an attitude of mind; the latter is a passing outward manifestation of this attitude." In my visit to the Anne Frank House, it was Anne's playfulness (not particular play activities) that made the biggest impression on me. When I think about Anne Frank, I certainly don't think about fun and games—but I do think about her playful way of engaging with the world.

I continued to think about Anne Frank's playfulness as I returned to the *Doors of Perception* conference. For the rest of the conference, I immersed myself in new video games and electronic toys. But when it came time for the final panel of the conference, I didn't talk about those innovative technologies. Instead, I explained how I had learned more about the essence of play and playfulness from Anne Frank than from any of the new technologies at the conference.

PLAYPENS AND PLAYGROUNDS

People use the word *play* in many ways. They play games, they play sports. They play musical instruments, they play songs. They play the odds, they play the stock market. They play with toys, they play with ideas.

What do people learn as they engage in these different types of play? Some parents and educators are skeptical about the connection between play and learning, dismissing playful activities as *just play*. Researchers sometimes go to the opposite extreme. I once went to a conference called *Play = Learning*, implying that all types of play lead to valuable learning experiences.

In my mind, not all types of play are created equal. Some types of play lead to creative learning experiences; others don't. We need to ask: What types of play are most likely to help young people develop as creative thinkers? And how can we best encourage and support those types of play?

I like the metaphor suggested by Marina Bers, a professor of child development at Tufts University. Marina notes that there is a big difference between playpens and playgrounds: Both are designed to support play, but they support different types of play—and different types of learning.

A *playpen* is a restrictive environment. In actual playpens, children have limited room to move and limited opportunities to explore. Children play with toys in playpens, but the range of possibilities is limited. In her book *Designing Digital Experiences for Positive Youth Development*, Marina explains that she uses the playpen "as a metaphor that conveys lack of freedom to experiment, lack of autonomy for exploration, lack of creative opportunities, and lack of risks."

In contrast, a *playground* provides children with more room to move, explore, experiment, and collaborate. Watch children on a playground, and you'll inevitably see them making up their own activities and games. In the process, children develop as creative thinkers. As Marina describes it: "The playground promotes, while the playpen hinders, a sense of mastery, creativity, self-confidence, and open exploration." This is especially true of modern "adventure playgrounds," which are explicitly designed to engage children in building, creating, and experimenting.

One reason that I've always been attracted to LEGO bricks is that they are well-suited for playground-style play. Give children a bucket of LEGO bricks, and they can build almost anything they can imagine, from houses to castles, from dogs to dragons, from cars to spaceships. Then, they can take apart their creations and make something new—in an endless flow of creative activity, just like children creating new games and activities on a playground.

But that's not the only way that children play with LEGO bricks. When some children play with LEGO bricks, they follow step-by-step building instructions to make the model that's featured on the front of the LEGO box. They build Hogwarts Castle from *Harry Potter*, or they build the Millennium Falcon from *Star Wars*. After they finish building, they put their finished model on display on a shelf in their room. These children are playing in the LEGO playpen, not the LEGO playground. They are learning how to follow instructions, but they aren't developing to their full potential as creative thinkers.

Of course, there is nothing wrong with providing children with some structure for their activities. Images of sample projects on the LEGO box offer one type of structure, providing inspiration and ideas for children as they get started. By following step-by-step LEGO building instructions, children can gain expertise with the materials, learning new techniques for building structures and mechanisms. Completing a complex model can be an enjoyable and satisfying experience, for all ages. But if the goal is creative thinking, then step-by-step instructions should be a stepping stone, not a final destination. For playground-style play, it's important for children to make the decisions about what to make and how to make it.

When we organize workshops for kids, we always try to support playground-style play. We provide various structures to help kids get started. For a LEGO robotics workshop, for example, we'll usually suggest a theme for the workshop, like "Underwater Adventure" or "Interactive Garden," to help spark ideas and encourage collaboration among workshop participants. We'll also show sample mechanisms that demonstrate different types of motion and provide a sense of what's possible. But we feel it's important for kids in the workshop to come up with their own ideas and plans. In an Interactive Garden workshop, for example, a child might imagine, then create, a robotic flower that closes its petals when something approaches. We want kids to experience the challenges and joys of turning their own ideas into projects. That's the essence of playground-style play.

In recent years, children have started spending more of their playtime on computer screens. This opens new opportunities for creative play and creative learning, but many of the new on-screen play activities feel more like playpens than playgrounds. Even the LEGO Group, with its long history of playground-style play in the physical world, has focused primarily on playpen-style activities on the screen. The company has produced an extensive collection of video games, many of them themed around movies and comic-book characters. The games definitely have a LEGO visual look: the objects and scenery are made of virtual LEGO bricks, and the characters are LEGO minifigures. But the style of play is very different from playing with a bucket of (physical) LEGO bricks. In the video games, kids learn to navigate through virtual worlds to score points and advance levels. But the games offer kids few opportunities to imagine new possibilities, set their own goals, or invent their own activities. In short, the games feel more like playpens than playgrounds.

It doesn't have to be that way. There can be playgrounds on the screen, just as in the physical world. The wild popularity and success of Minecraft is largely due to its playground-style approach. With Minecraft, kids can build their own (virtual) structures, craft their own tools, invent their own games. There is a wide variety of different ways to play with Minecraft. Although Minecraft (virtual) blocks don't look like LEGO (physical) blocks, the play patterns are very similar.

Our Scratch software is another type of on-screen playground. Our original tagline for Scratch was "imagine, program, share." People often associate Scratch with programming, but imagining and sharing are just as important to the Scratch experience. Just as kids on a playground are constantly making up new games to play with one another, kids on the Scratch website are constantly imagining new types of projects and sharing their creations with one another. Most other coding websites are designed as playpens, offering a constrained set of activities to help kids learn specific coding concepts. For us, the playground-style approach of Scratch is every bit as important as the computational ideas embedded in the programming blocks.

With so many different types of play—playing games, playing with toys, playing in playpens, playing on playgrounds—it's surprising that we have just a single word for play. But that's just a limitation of English. My colleague Amos Blanton, who worked on the Scratch Team at MIT before joining the LEGO Foundation in Denmark, was surprised to find that Danish has two different words for play. The word *spille* is used to describe the types of play that have a defined structure and sets of rules, like playing sports or playing a video game, whereas the word *lege* is used to describe play that is imaginative and open-ended, without an explicit goal. It seems appropriate that the Danish toy company is named LEGO (a contraction of *lege* with *godt*, meaning *play well*) and not SPILGO; LEGO bricks are explicitly designed to support imaginative, open-ended play.

Play is one of the four P's of creative learning. But to help children develop as creative thinkers, we need to distinguish between different types of play, putting more emphasis on lege than spille, and more emphasis on playgrounds than playpens.

TINKERING

When we were developing LEGO/Logo, the first LEGO robotics kit, we tested our initial prototypes in a fourth-grade class at an elementary school in Boston. One of the students, named Nicky, started by building a car out of LEGO bricks. After racing the car down a ramp several times, Nicky added a motor to the car and connected it to the computer. When he programmed the motor to turn on, the car moved forward a bit—but then the motor fell off the body of the car and began vibrating across the table on its own.

Rather than trying to repair the car, Nicky became intrigued with the vibration of the motor. He played and experimented with the vibrating motor, and began to wonder whether he might be able to use the vibrations to power a vehicle. Nicky mounted the motor on a platform atop four "legs" (LEGO axles). After some experimentation, Nicky realized that he needed some way to amplify the motor vibrations. To do that, he drew upon some personal experiences. Nicky enjoyed riding a skateboard, and he remembered that swinging his arms gave him an extra push on the skateboard. He figured that a swinging arm might accentuate the vibrations of the motor as well, so he connected two LEGO axles with a hinged joint to create an arm and attached it to the motor. As the motor turned, the arm whipped around—and amplified the motor vibrations, just as Nicky had hoped.

In fact, the system vibrated so strongly that it frequently tipped over. A classmate suggested that Nicky create a more stable base by placing a LEGO tire horizontally at the bottom of each leg. Nicky made the revision, and his "vibrating walker" worked perfectly. Nicky was even able to steer the walker. When he programmed the motor to turn in one direction, the walker vibrated forward and to the right. When he programmed the motor to turn in the other direction, the walker vibrated forward and to the left.

I was impressed with Nicky's vibrating walker—but even more impressed by the strategies he used in creating it. As Nicky worked on his project, he was constantly *tinkering*. Throughout the process, he was playfully experimenting, trying out new ideas, reassessing his goals, making refinements, and imagining new possibilities. Like all good tinkerers, Nicky was:

• *Taking advantage of the unexpected.* When the motor fell off of his car, Nicky didn't see it as a sign of failure; he saw it as an opportunity for new explorations.

• *Drawing on personal experience.* When Nicky needed to amplify the vibrations of the motor, he relied on his experiences as a skateboarder and knowledge of his own body.

- *Using familiar materials in unfamiliar ways.* Most people don't imagine LEGO axles as arms or legs, nor do they imagine LEGO wheels as feet—but Nicky was able to look at objects in the world around him and see them in new ways.

Tinkering is not a new idea. From the time the earliest humans began making and using tools, tinkering has been a valuable strategy for making things. But in today's fast-changing world, tinkering is more important than ever. Tinkerers understand how to improvise, adapt, and iterate, so they're never hung up on old plans as new situations arise. Tinkering breeds creativity.

Tinkering is at the intersection of playing and making. In the same way that many people are dismissive of the value of play (*just play*), many are also dismissive of the value of tinkering (*just tinkering*). Schools tend to emphasize the value of planning over tinkering. Planning seems more organized, more direct, more efficient. Planners take a *top-down* approach: They analyze a situation, identify needs, develop a clear plan, then execute it. Do it once and do it right. What could be better than that?

The tinkering process is messier. Tinkerers take a *bottom-up* approach: They start small, try out simple ideas, react to what happens, make adjustments, and refine their plans. They often take a meandering, circuitous path to get to a solution. But what they lose in efficiency they gain in creativity and agility. When unexpected things happen and when new opportunities arise, tinkerers are better positioned to take advantage. As Media Lab director Joi Ito likes to say: "You don't get lucky if you plan everything."

Tinkerers constantly reevaluate their goals (where they're going) and their plans (how to get there). Sometimes, tinkerers start without a goal. They spend time messing around with materials, playfully exploring what's possible, until a goal emerges from their explorations. Other times, they start with a general goal (Nicky was planning to make a car), but are quick to adjust their goals and plans as new things happen (the motor fell off and vibrated across the table).

"When you tinker, you're not following a step-by-step set of directions that leads you to a tidy end result," write Karen Wilkinson and Mike Petrich, in their wonderful book *The Art of Tinkering*. "Instead, you're questioning your assumptions about the way something works, and you're investigating it on your own terms. You're giving yourself permission to fiddle with this and dabble with that. And chances are, you're also blowing your own mind."

Tinkerers believe in rapid prototyping and iteration. When working on a design project, they build something quickly, try it out, get reactions from other people, then make a new version— over and over. Tinkerers prefer to use screws, not nails. They're constantly making changes and revisions. When they're solving problems, they come up with a quick solution, something that sort-of works, then look for ways to improve it.

As we work on new projects in my research group, we're always tinkering—making new prototypes, testing them out, revising them, over and over. We developed dozens of prototypes of programmable bricks before the LEGO Group decided to move forward with LEGO Mindstorms as a product. Some prototypes proved to be dead ends; we backtracked and tried other options. Similarly, as we worked on Scratch, we constantly tried out new designs: How should the programming blocks fit together? How should the objects communicate with one another? We worked on one prototype after another—and we continue to tinker with the design of Scratch today.

Many of the greatest scientists and engineers throughout history—from Leonardo da Vinci to Alexander Graham Bell to Barbara McClintock to Richard Feynman—saw themselves as tinkerers. People often assume that all scientists are planners, because scientific papers make it seem as though every step was carefully planned in advance. But studies of scientists working in their labs reveal that scientists do a lot more tinkering than they describe in their papers.

Still, many educators remain skeptical about tinkering. There are several common critiques. Some educators worry that tinkerers might succeed at creating things without fully understanding what they're doing. That might be true in some cases. But even in those cases, tinkering provides an opportunity for learners to develop fragments of knowledge that they can later integrate into a more complete understanding.

Educators also worry that tinkering is too unstructured—that it doesn't provide the systematicity and rigor needed for success. This critique misunderstands the true nature of tinkering. The *bottom-up* process of tinkering starts with explorations that might seem rather random, but it doesn't end there. True tinkerers know how to turn their initial explorations (*bottom*) into a focused activity (*up*). Nicky spent a lot of time playing and experimenting with a vibrating motor (*bottom*) and then used his newly gained insights to create a walking machine powered by vibrations (*up*). It's a problem if learners get stuck only on the *bottom*; it's the combination of *bottom* and *up* that makes tinkering a valuable process.

People often associate tinkering with physical construction— building a castle with LEGO bricks, constructing a tree house with wood, creating a circuit with electronic components. The Maker

Movement has reinforced this image, because it usually focuses on making things in the physical world. But I see tinkering as an approach to making things, regardless of whether the things are physical or virtual. You can tinker when you're writing a story or programming an animation. The key issue is your style of interaction, not the media or materials that you use.

We explicitly designed our Scratch programming language to encourage tinkering. It's easy to snap together Scratch's graphical programming blocks and also easy to take them apart, just like LEGO bricks. To try out a stack of Scratch blocks, you just click on it, and it executes immediately—no waiting for code to compile. You can even make changes to the code as it's running. It's easy to quickly put together a little project, play with it, modify it, extend it—and you can enhance your project by pulling in images, photos, and sounds from the Internet, just as physical world tinkerers mix together materials from the world around them.

We need to provide children with more opportunities to tinker, with both physical and digital materials. The tinkering process can be messy and meandering, but that's true of all creative processes. A careful plan can lead to efficient results, but you can't plan your way to creativity. Creative thinking grows out of creative tinkering.

MANY PATHS, MANY STYLES

In the chapter on passion (the second of the 4 P's), I emphasized the importance of wide walls. In addition to providing children with easy ways to get started on projects (low floors) and ways for them to work on increasingly sophisticated projects over time (high ceilings), we also need to support many different pathways between the floor and the ceiling (wide walls). Why? Different children have different interests and passions, so they'll want to work on different types of projects. When children work with Scratch, for example, some want to create platform games, some want to create dance animations, some want to create interactive newsletters: Our wide walls strategy aims to support all of them.

There's another reason for wide walls. Children differ from one another not only in their interests and passions, but also in the ways they play and learn. If we want to help all children develop as creative thinkers, we need to support all types of play styles and learning styles.

The diversity of play and learning styles became obvious to us as we started testing our initial LEGO robotics kits in elementary-school classrooms. In one class, we asked the students what types of projects they wanted to work on, and they decided to create an amusement park, with different groups of students working on different rides for the park.

One group of three students immediately began working on a merry-go-round. They carefully drew up plans, then used LEGO bricks, beams, and gears to build the structure and mechanisms. After they finished building the merry-go-round, they wrote a computer program to make it spin around, then added a touch sensor to control it. Whenever anyone touched the sensor, the merry-go-round would spin in one direction, then the other. The group experimented with different computer programs, varying how long the merry-go-round rotated in each direction. The whole project, from initial idea to final implementation, took just a couple of hours.

Another group, also with three students, decided to build a Ferris wheel. But after working for 30 minutes on the basic structure for the Ferris wheel, they put it aside and started building a refreshment stand next to the Ferris wheel. At first I was concerned. Part of the purpose of the activity was for students to learn about gearing mechanisms and computer programming. If they built only refreshment stands, without any gears or motors or sensors, they would miss out on important learning experiences. But I knew it was best not to intervene too quickly.

After finishing the refreshment stand, the students built a wall around the entire amusement park. Then, they created a parking lot, and added lots of miniature LEGO people walking into the park. They developed an elaborate story about several families coming from different parts of the city to spend a day at the amusement park. Only then, after the whole amusement-park scene was complete, did the students go back and finish building and programming their Ferris wheel. To them, building the Ferris wheel wasn't interesting until they had imagined a story around it.

In one study of how children interact with their toys, Dennie Wolf and Howard Gardner identified two primary styles of play. They described some children as *patterners* and others as *dramatists*. Patterners are fascinated by structures and patterns, and they typically enjoy playing with blocks and puzzles. Dramatists are more interested in stories and social interaction, and they often play with dolls and stuffed animals.

In the amusement park workshop, members of the first group would be classified as patterners. Their focus was on making the merry-go-round work, then experimenting with different patterns of behavior. Members of the second group would be classified as dramatists. They were interested in their Ferris wheel only when it was part of a story. The two groups were working with the same materials, learning similar things about gearing mechanisms and computer programming, but they had very different styles of playing and learning.

This variation in styles is not unique to elementary school students. It can be seen in learners of all ages, including university students. While we were developing the first programmable bricks in the early 1990s, two graduate students in our research group, Fred Martin and Randy Sargent, started a Robot Design Competition for MIT students. The competition has become an annual event. Every January, during the intersession between semesters, teams of MIT students spend four weeks—often working around the clock, with little sleep—to design, build, and program robots to compete against one another in specified tasks, such as gathering ping-pong balls or navigating mazes. At the end of the month, hundreds of spectators pack into the largest auditorium on campus to watch the finals of the competition.

Two faculty members at Wellesley College, Robbie Berg and Franklyn Turbak, were impressed with the MIT event, and decided to organize a similar activity for Wellesley students. But they felt that a robot competition wouldn't attract the same level of interest among students at Wellesley, an all-women liberal arts college. Instead, they organized a course called the *Robotic Design Studio*, with a somewhat different approach. Like the MIT Robot Design Competition, the Wellesley Robotic Design Studio is a month-long immersive experience, and participating students use similar robotics technology. But instead of creating robots for a competition, the Wellesley students have built a diverse collection of artistic and expressive creations, such as a robotic version of a scene from the Wizard of Oz. At the end of the month, instead of a competition, there is an exhibition of the students' robotic inventions—much like the opening of a new exhibition at an art gallery.

The Wellesley Robotic Design Studio has a different feel from the MIT Robot Design Competition. The Wellesley course seems more suited for dramatists; the MIT course seems more suited for patterners. But the results are similar. Both courses are extremely popular, and students in both courses learn important science and engineering concepts and skills.

Math and science courses, from elementary school through college, have traditionally been designed in ways that favor patterners over dramatists—just as they tend to favor planners over tinkerers. That's a big reason why many kids get turned off by math and science. Dramatists and tinkerers often get the message that math and science aren't for them. It doesn't have to be that way. The problem isn't in the disciplines themselves, but in how they're presented and taught. Sherry Turkle and Seymour Papert coined the term "epistemological pluralism" to highlight the importance of accepting, valuing, and supporting many different ways of knowing.

As my research group at the Media Lab develops new technologies and activities, we're constantly looking for ways to support many paths and many styles. For the amusement park workshop, we provided students with not just gears, motors, and sensors (as would be typical in robotics workshops), but also miniature LEGO people and a wide range of craft materials (such as construction paper, pom-poms, and glitter). These additional materials were essential to creating the day-at-the-park story that motivated the dramatists on the Ferris wheel team.

It's also important to provide learners with sufficient time, because some paths and styles take longer than others. What if the amusement park workshop had ended after an hour? At that point, the first team (the patterners) had already completed a fully functioning merry-go-round, with a computer program to control its motions. The second team (the dramatists) had built only part of a Ferris wheel and a refreshment stand. If the workshop had ended then, the patterners probably would have been viewed as much more successful than the dramatists. Fortunately, there was additional time for the Ferris wheel team to continue developing its day-at-the-park story, then finish building and programming the Ferris wheel.

Learners differ from one another in many ways: Some are patterners, others are dramatists; some are planners, others are tinkerers; some prefer to express themselves through text, others through images. Many people wonder whether these differences result from nature or nurture—that is, whether styles are inborn or based on experience in the world. For me, that's not the most interesting or important issue. Rather, we should focus on figuring out ways to help all children, of all backgrounds and learning styles, reach their full potential. How can we develop technologies, activities, and courses that engage and support all different types of learners?

At the same time, we should push learners to reach outside their comfort zone. For certain types of problems, planning has advantages over tinkering; for other types of problems, tinkering has advantages. Exploring patterns is particularly helpful in some situations; telling stories is particularly helpful in other situations. Even if an individual learner is more comfortable with one style over another, it's useful to experiment with other styles and approaches. Ideally, all children should have the opportunity to engage with the world in a style that's most natural and comfortable for them— but also have experience with other styles, so that they can shift strategies as the situation warrants.

TRY, TRY AGAIN

In looking at projects on the Scratch website, I became intrigued by projects created by a community member with the username EmeraldDragon. My interest wasn't so much in the projects themselves (many of which, not surprisingly, feature dragons), but rather the way in which EmeraldDragon created the projects.

In one of her first projects, EmeraldDragon created a game in which a user can control the movements of an animated dragon. She created 12 images of a dragon, each with the dragon's legs in slightly different positions, then created a programming script that cycled through the images to create the appearance of motion, much like a flipbook. EmeraldDragon experimented with different versions of the script to make the dragon move in different directions when the user pressed different keys.

When EmeraldDragon shared the project on the Scratch website, she included this comment: "I was just tinkering with the scripts in the game and I finally figured out how to make it so you can run back and forth! I'll fix up the game and put out the new and improved still not yet a game version!" EmeraldDragon named her project *My Dragon Game (NOT finished)*, to make clear that the project was still a work-in-progress. In her project notes, she wrote: "I am working on being able to run back and forth without the rock disappearing. Any tips or help?"

In the project's comments section, other members of the Scratch community offered suggestions on how to fix the problem. EmeraldDragon made changes to the project and shared an improved version, but she still wasn't satisfied with the project. This time, she gave it the name *My Dragon Game (Still NOT finished)*. In her project notes, she wrote: "This is just a stage in a long process."

Many children get discouraged or frustrated when they can't get things to work right away. But not EmeraldDragon. She wasn't afraid to make mistakes. For her, mistakes were part of the process. When at first she didn't succeed, she was eager to try, try again. She continued to ask for advice and suggestions from others in the community, and she continued to seek new strategies for revising and improving her project.

This type of attitude is critical to the creative process. In his popular TED Talks on creativity, Sir Ken Robinson emphasizes the importance of taking risks and making mistakes. "If you're not prepared to be wrong, you'll never come up with anything original," he explains. "We're running education systems where mistakes are the worst thing you can make. We're educating people out of their creative capacities."

Instead, to help kids develop as creative thinkers, we need to create environments where kids feel comfortable making mistakes—and where they can learn from their mistakes. That's one reason I'm so excited about kids learning to code. Compared with many other activities, coding tends to be more forgiving. If you cut a piece of wood in half or nail two pieces of wood together, it's often difficult to make adjustments afterwards. With coding, it's easier to undo whatever you've done. It's easier to recover from mistakes, make adjustments, and try something new.

There's a tradition among programmers to see mistakes not as a sign of failure but as "bugs" that can be fixed. An important part of becoming a programmer is to learn strategies for *debugging*—that is, how to identify and isolate a problem, then make changes to get around the problem. The debugging process is hardly unique to coding. Indeed, when kids learn to code, the strategies they learn for debugging their programs are useful for all types of problem-solving and design activities. But coding is a particularly good context for learning and practicing debugging, because it's quick and easy to make changes to programs and try them out.

With Scratch, some debugging strategies are social. As Emerald-Dragon did with her dragon game, kids can reach out to others in the online community for advice and suggestions. Some kids are hesitant to share projects while they're still working out the bugs, worrying that others in the community might make comments that are overly critical. To make kids feel more comfortable sharing their works-in-progress, we added a new feature to Scratch, allowing kids to indicate that a project is a draft. By labeling a project as a draft, kids can regulate what others in the community expect from the project, while also making it clear that they're looking for feedback and advice on the project.

For some kids, experiences with Scratch have fundamentally changed the way they think about mistakes and failure. In a television segment about Africa Code Week, a teenage Scratcher explained it like this: "For me personally, it's been a way to embrace making mistakes, and get rid of that fear of failure, because failure is so important in programming. Getting something wrong is like the best thing that you can do because it leads to either solving that challenge—or the computer does something weird that I didn't expect, and I like it, and then I'm pursuing that."

This way of thinking aligns with what psychologist Carol Dweck has termed a *growth mindset*. According to Dweck, people with a growth mindset see intelligence as malleable, and they recognize that they can continue to learn and develop through hard work and dedication. As a result, they're willing to embrace challenges, persist in the face of setbacks, and learn from their mistakes. By contrast, people with a *fixed mindset* see intelligence as a fixed trait. They're likely to view mistakes as a sign of their own inherent inadequacy, and thus they tend to avoid challenges and give up easily.

As my research group develops new technologies and activities, we're always trying to promote and support a growth mindset. Through our design of the Scratch programming environment and our management of the Scratch online community, we try to make it easy and comfortable for kids to try new things, take risks, ask questions when they're stuck, experiment with new strategies when things go wrong, and support one another in their ongoing explorations.

So, it makes us happy to see blog posts like this one, from a mother reflecting on her daughter's experience with Scratch: "It has afforded her a bravery to try new things. Even if the first result is failure, that failure is only a clue to an alternate path that should be taken instead of an end to the quest, and there are multiple paths that could lead to the same destination, not always a 'right' and 'wrong' way."

TENSIONS AND TRADE-OFFS: ASSESSMENT

Our colleagues at the Exploratorium published a paper called "It Looks Like Fun, but Are They Learning?" We often hear similar questions about our activities. Sure, a playful approach seems nice, but what are children gaining from the experience? These questions point to one of the biggest challenges in our efforts to cultivate creativity: How can we assess what children are learning?

To explore these questions, let me start with a story about learning, creativity, and assessment in the island nation of Singapore. Students in Singapore have consistently ranked near the top of the world in standardized international exams, such as Program for International Student Assessment (PISA) and Trends in International Mathematics and Science Study (TIMSS)—and educators and government officials are understandably proud of their nation's high ranking in these exams.

But there's a problem. As Singapore businesses have moved into more creative activities over the past couple of decades, they've found that graduates from Singapore high schools are no longer meeting their needs. One Singapore business executive explained that new employees perform well when they're given well-defined tasks that match what they learned in school. But as soon as unexpected situations arise, many new employees—even those with high scores on the international exams—aren't able to adapt and figure out new strategies for dealing with the new challenges.

In response, the Singapore Ministry of Education has tried to introduce changes in the schools to encourage more creative thinking. Schools are experimenting with new teaching strategies in an effort to move away from the drill-and-practice, rote-learning approach that had been common in many Singapore classrooms.

On one of my visits to Singapore, a ministry representative took me to a school where students were building and programming their own robots, using the LEGO Mindstorms robotics kit. The students showed me the robots they'd created for a nationwide robotics competition and demonstrated how they had programmed their robots to navigate through a maze. I suggested some new tasks for the robots, and the students quickly reprogrammed their robots, coming up with creative solutions to the challenges. I was impressed. The students had clearly learned some engineering skills—and more importantly (at least to me), they were developing as creative thinkers.

Before leaving the school, I talked with the students' teacher and asked how she had integrated the robotics activities into the classroom curriculum. She looked at me with a shocked expression, as if I'd asked a crazy question. "Oh no," she said. "We would never do these activities during the school day. Students work on their robotics projects after school. During school hours, they need to focus on their lessons."

The teacher was proud of her students' accomplishments in the national robotics competition, and she knew that the government was encouraging these types of activities to help students develop as creative thinkers. Still, the teacher couldn't imagine bringing the robotics activities into the classroom during the school day. She needed to focus on the core subjects to prepare students for exams.

Although this story involves a particular teacher and a particular set of activities, it points to a more general dilemma: How can we encourage and support creativity in an era when standardized exams set the agenda for classroom activities? In many places, standardized exams even set the agenda for children's lives outside of school, as parents sign up children for special after-school courses to help prepare for exams.

There are some good arguments for standardized exams. There's a need for accountability (are tax dollars being well spent?), feedback for teachers (are their teaching methods working well?), and feedback for students (do they have misunderstandings and misconceptions?).

But are standardized exams measuring the right things? Exams might be able to measure how well students can do arithmetic problems or how well they've learned certain dates in history or how well they can follow instructions. But are exams capable of measuring the things that will make the biggest difference in children's lives? In particular, can they measure students' ability to think creatively?

Some critics have compared the use of standardized exams to the person who loses their keys on a dark street, then looks for the keys near the streetlight because it's easier to search there. Schools don't know how to measure creative thinking, so they end up measuring things that they can measure more easily. Some of those measures can be useful, but they end up distorting priorities. There's an old saying "We treasure what we measure." Schools tend to focus more attention, and place more value, on the things that they can measure, rather than valuing and focusing on the things that will make the biggest difference in children's lives.

There are efforts now to develop better quantitative measures of creative thinking (and other skills and competencies that have been traditionally difficult to measure). In today's data-obsessed world, some people think that everything can be quantitatively measured, if we just figure out the right data to collect. I'm skeptical. As sociologist William Bruce Cameron once wrote: "Not everything that can be counted counts, and not everything that counts can be counted."

There is a lot of talk these days about "evidence-based" practices in education—meaning that we should decide how and what to teach based on evidence, and we should assess students' progress based on evidence. I certainly agree that we should value evidence. But people too often focus only on quantitative evidence, expressed in numbers and statistics. That's a problem. If we want to support things that are the most valuable and important (such as creative thinking and the joy of learning), we need to broaden our view of evidence. Rather than just trying to *measure* what children learn (through numbers), we also need to *document* what children learn (through compelling examples). Rather than trying to assess what children have learned by giving them an exam with right/wrong answers, we should work with children to document their projects, illustrating what they created, how they created it, and why. Teachers and others can then review these portfolios and provide children with suggestions and feedback about their projects and learning process.

Most school systems, and most people, don't take portfolio-based approaches as seriously as "hard numbers." In K–12 education, portfolios are sometimes denigrated as a "soft" approach to assessment. But portfolios and non-quantitative forms of evidence have proven to be very successful in other contexts. Consider the process that was used when I was evaluated for promotion as a faculty member at MIT. No one gave me an exam. No one performed a quantitative analysis of my research contributions. Instead, I was asked to put together a portfolio with examples of my research.

Then, MIT asked experts in my field to review my portfolio and provide feedback on the significance and creativity of my research contributions.

When we admit students to our graduate program at the MIT Media Lab, we also focus on portfolios and non-quantitative forms of assessment. Applicants aren't required to submit any standardized test scores. Although applicants are asked to submit transcripts with their college grades, I rarely look at them. Instead, I look at the project portfolios and research statements, in which the applicants describe why they worked on their projects, what they learned, and what they want to do next.

This emphasis on non-quantitative assessment fits well with the Media Lab's focus on creativity and innovation. It's not easy to measure creativity and innovation quantitatively, so we need to rely on different approaches for assessment. If portfolios and other non-quantitative approaches are good enough for the Media Lab, why not for K–12 schools too?

I'm not suggesting that there are easy answers on how to assess K–12 students. Many of the approaches that we use at the Media Lab aren't easy to scale up, so they couldn't necessarily be used for assessing large numbers of students. But the continuing K–12 focus on testing and measurement is distorting the priorities and practices of educators, researchers, and parents. If we truly care about preparing today's children to thrive in tomorrow's society, we need to rethink our approaches to assessment, making sure to focus on what's most important for children to learn, not what's easiest for us to measure.

IN THEIR OWN VOICES: JIMMY

As a child, Jimmy regularly went to the Computer Clubhouse next to his school in Costa Rica. Now 29 years old, Jimmy works as an engineer for IBM in Costa Rica.

Me: How did you get started at the Computer Clubhouse?

Jimmy: I saw the Computer Clubhouse, and I was very curious. My parents didn't have money to buy me LEGO sets. I asked the Clubhouse coordinator, "How much do I have to pay to come use the LEGO sets at the Clubhouse?" He said: "No, it's free for you." I thought: Are you kidding me? Then he showed me the LEGO Mindstorms robotics kit. I opened that box, and it changed everything. I could keep learning and learning, and it was free.

Me: It seems that you had a passion for building things from an early age. Where did that come from?

Jimmy: My dad was a carpenter, so he taught me how to build little things with wood. I learned in those days that it was easy for me to use my hands to build things. I remember that I built little cars with bottle caps and little squares of wood. And I used bottles, paper, plastic, gum, and other things to form little robots. They didn't move, they were just little figures, but that's how I got started with robots, before going to the Computer Clubhouse.

Me: What types of robots did you build at the Clubhouse?

Jimmy: When I was growing up, I liked dinosaurs. I can remember the T. rex dinosaur I invented with two legs. I was the kind of child who didn't want to use wheels. I thought: Why do I have to use wheels? I want to use legs. I studied pictures of different animals. How did the animals move their legs? I was 12 years old or less, and that was my first biped robot. After that, I developed many different biped robots.

I also remember building a monkey that moved with its arms. We put a string across the room, and the monkey could walk along the string, putting one arm over the next. I thought: Why do I need wheels to get from one side to another?

I also built a machine to sort LEGO bricks based on their color. It had a little arm that pushed LEGO bricks this way or that way, and it used a sensor that I took out of a printer. To develop the code was a big challenge for me. It took me many weeks.

Me: As you worked on projects at the Clubhouse, how did you learn the things you needed to learn?

Jimmy: When I started building robots at the Clubhouse, I started by playing with pulleys and gears. I kept trying new things to see what would work. I learned how you can put a little gear with a big gear to get a low speed or a faster speed. And the Clubhouse had books that showed different mechanisms. I remember a book showing drawings from Leonardo da Vinci.

Then, I needed to learn how to program the robots. I didn't know anything about it. I started by programming in Logo, with the little turtle. By programming that little turtle, I learned how to put my mind in the logic of code. After the Clubhouse, I used that same logic to learn C++ and Java and Python, but it all started with Logo, with the little turtle, at the Clubhouse.

I learned a lot by working with other Clubhouse members. We were always sharing ideas. When I went to the Clubhouse Teen Summit, I got a chance to work with children from many different countries, from all over the world. That was very new to me. I shared ideas with other children, they shared ideas with me, and together we could build a better robot.

Me: How did your Clubhouse experiences prepare you for your current job at IBM?

Jimmy: Many doors have been opened for me because of the Clubhouse. I studied electronics in college, and now I'm working as an engineer at IBM here in Costa Rica. In my job, I work together with people from many different countries, just like I did at the Clubhouse Teen Summit.

At the Clubhouse, I learned that you can create things if you put your mind, your heart, and your passion into it. It's not just the technology, it's the philosophy. At the Clubhouse, I learned to share, share, share: share information, share technology, share what you learn.

Me: What are your plans for the future?

Jimmy: Outside of my job at IBM, I'm developing robots using Scratch, Arduino, and LEGO WeDo. I'm planning to start a website, where children can download building instructions, including the Scratch code, totally free, with alternative constructions and robots.

Many of the things I learned at the Computer Clubhouse I want to teach to others. I like to say that technology is not the end: It is a bridge to help others. I want to help other children learn the way I learned at the Clubhouse. I can't keep my knowledge only for me. Everything that I've learned, I want to put to serve others.

6

CREATIVE SOCIETY

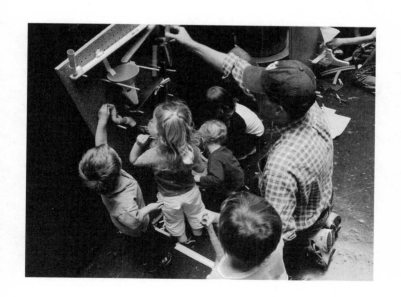

A HUNDRED LANGUAGES

In the past few decades, there has been much talk about the transition from an *industrial society* to an *information society*. People now see information, not natural resources, as the driving force in the economy and society. Others prefer to describe our current era as a *knowledge society*, noting that information is useful only when it's transformed into knowledge.

In this book, I've been making the case for a different framework: the *creative society*. As the pace of change in the world continues to accelerate, people must learn how to adapt to constantly changing conditions. Success in the future—for individuals, for communities, for companies, for nations as a whole—will be based on the ability to think and act creatively.

The shift to a creative society presents both a need and an opportunity. There is a pressing need to help young people develop as creative thinkers so that they're prepared for life in a fast-changing world. At the same time, we can use this transition as an opportunity to promote a more humane set of values in society. One of the best ways to help young people prepare for life in a creative society is to make sure that they have the chance to follow their interests, to explore their ideas, to develop their voices. Those are values I would have wanted in any era, but they're more important now than ever before.

To take advantage of this opportunity, and to nurture these values, we need to pull together people from all parts of society: parents, teachers, designers, policymakers, and children. How can we do that? One place where I've looked for ideas and inspiration is the small Italian city of Reggio Emilia, which has developed a network of preschools and kindergartens that provide a glimpse into the possibilities of the creative society.

At the heart of the Reggio approach is a deep respect for the abilities of the child. The schools are designed to support and document children's explorations and investigations. On one visit to a Reggio classroom, I saw a table full of magnifying glasses, microscopes, and webcams that children were using to examine the microstructure of lettuce and other vegetables. On another table was an incredible assortment of crayons, markers, and craft materials that children were using to draw scenes from the city—and then to build models based on their drawings. In another classroom, children were studying worms that they found in the field next to the school, and they were making a long list of things they were learning about worms.

In Reggio classrooms, children and teachers are constantly documenting their work—and posting their documentation on the walls of the classroom for everyone to see. It's part of a process that they call *making learning visible.* The documentation serves several purposes: It encourages children to reflect upon their work, it enables teachers to get a better understanding of their students' thinking, and it provides a way for parents (when they visit the classroom) to see what their children have been working on. Parents are viewed as partners and collaborators, invited to participate in all parts of the educational process.

Some of the documentation is published in book form so that teachers, parents, and researchers around the world can learn from the experiences in Reggio. One book documents children's exploration of shadows. The book is full of photographs of children creating and playing with shadows, exploring how different types of objects cast different types of shadows and how shadows change over the course of the day. It also includes children's drawings of shadows and their explanations of how shadows work. The book has a delightful title, based on a quote from one of the children: *Everything Has a Shadow Except Ants.*

Often, teams of children become engaged in long-term collaborative projects. On my first visit to Reggio, in 1999, one kindergarten class was involved in a year-long project to design new curtains for the city's opera house, located a few blocks from their school. The children spent several weeks at the opera house, studying it inside and out. They decided that their curtain design should include plants and bugs, in part because of their interest in the plants around the opera house, and in part because of their interest in the movie *A Bug's Life*, which had recently been released. Working with their teachers, they explored ideas around transformation and metamorphosis: how seeds turn into plants, how caterpillars turn into butterflies.

The children created hundreds of drawings of plants and bugs, scanned them into a computer, manipulated and combined the drawings, and produced large-scale copies. Toward the end of the year, they again spent several weeks at the opera house, painting their images onto the curtain. The project was an example of how Reggio children become actively involved in the life of the community. In another project, children designed and created bird fountains for the parks in Reggio. "Children are full citizens from the moment of birth," says Carla Rinaldi, who has led many educational initiatives at Reggio. In Reggio, it not only takes a village to raise a child, it also takes children to raise the village.

Loris Malaguzzi laid the foundation for the Reggio approach, working in the Reggio schools from the 1960s to the 1990s. One of Malaguzzi's core ideas was that children have many different ways of exploring the world and expressing themselves. In his poem "The Hundred Languages," Malaguzzi wrote:

The child has
a hundred languages
a hundred hands
a hundred thoughts
a hundred ways of thinking
of playing, of speaking.

Malaguzzi was critical of the way that most schools constrain children's imagination and creativity:

The child has
a hundred languages
(and a hundred hundred hundred more)
but they steal ninety-nine.
The school and the culture
separate the head from the body.
They tell the child:
to think without hands
to do without head
to listen and not to speak
to understand without joy
to love and to marvel
only at Easter and at Christmas.

Malaguzzi developed his ideas primarily for children in preschool and kindergarten, but the Reggio approach is valid for learners of all ages. We need to support a hundred languages (or more) for everyone, everywhere.

It's not easy to put these ideas into practice. John Dewey, the pioneer of the progressive education movement, wrote that his approach was "simple but not easy." That is, Dewey's ideas were relatively easy to describe, but difficult to implement. The same is true for the Reggio approach—and for the four P's of creative learning.

The path to the creative society isn't easy or straightforward. We need to engage many people in many ways. In the next three sections, I provide tips for supporting and participating in the movement toward a creative society—as a learner, a parent, a teacher, a designer, or a developer.

TEN TIPS FOR LEARNERS

As kids work on projects, they learn specific skills for using particular tools and technologies—but more important, they learn general strategies for working on creative projects. For this section, I started to compile a list of these creative learning strategies. But as I looked through some old notes, I came across a list of strategies that had been generated by a group of kids—and I liked their list more than my own! I decided to use their list as the framework for this section.

The list came from a workshop at the Boston Museum of Science, organized by Bakhtiar Mikhak. At the workshop, a group of 12-year-olds used some of our prototype robotics technologies to create interactive inventions. At the end of the day, after the kids had demonstrated and discussed their projects, Bakhtiar asked them to write down tips for kids who would be participating in a similar workshop the next day. Here are the tips that the kids generated (along with my own commentary on each tip).

1. START SIMPLE

This tip might seem obvious, but it's surprising how often people ignore it. When beginners start a Scratch project, they'll often build up a large set of complex scripts—without even trying any of them to see what they do. When I'm making a Scratch project, I always start with a simple script, make sure it works the way I want, then add to it incrementally, testing (and revising) each new version along the way. When I'm coordinating a workshop, I encourage participants to follow a similar strategy: Start with something simple, try it out, then keep extending and improving it. That strategy applies not just for Scratch projects, but for all types of projects.

2. WORK ON THINGS THAT YOU LIKE

My colleague Natalie Rusk likes to say that "interests are a natural resource that fuels learning." When you work on projects you care about, you're willing to work longer and harder and persist in the face of challenges. You're also motivated to learn new things. Natalie points to her younger brother as an example: He loved music as a child, which motivated him not only to learn to play musical instruments, but also to learn about electronics and the physics of sound (so that he could record, amplify, and manipulate music and sounds). The connection between learning and motivation goes in both directions. As the Irish poet W. B. Yeats wrote: "Education is not the filling of a pail but the lighting of a fire."

3. IF YOU HAVE NO CLUE WHAT TO DO, FIDDLE AROUND

It can feel intimidating when you're starting on a new project—somewhat like staring at a blank sheet of paper, not knowing what you want to write. Don't worry: It's OK not to have a goal or a plan as you're getting started. Sometimes, the best ideas arise through tinkering. Try using your tools and materials in new ways. Use familiar materials in unfamiliar ways. Use unfamiliar materials in familiar ways. Do something silly or whimsical with the materials. If something captures your attention, focus on it and explore it. Let your curiosity be your guide. By following your curiosity, you'll ultimately come up with new goals and plans—and you might even discover new passions.

4. DON'T BE AFRAID TO EXPERIMENT

It's useful to learn to follow instructions. If you follow instructions well, you'll be able to assemble IKEA furniture, you'll be able to cook a good meal, and you'll probably do well in school. On the other hand, if you *always* follow instructions—and if you *only* follow instructions—you'll never do anything very creative or innovative, and you'll get stuck when you encounter a new situation in which the instructions no longer apply. To become a creative thinker, you must be willing to experiment, to try new things, to ignore conventional wisdom. When you make modifications to a food recipe, there's a chance that you'll end up with a failed dinner, but there's also a chance that you'll come up with a creative new dish.

5. FIND A FRIEND TO WORK WITH AND SHARE IDEAS

There are many different ways to work with other people. You might collaborate directly on a project, or you might just share ideas and each work on your own project. You might get inspiration from someone without even talking with them. You might join a small group or participate in a large team. You might be the leader of the group or just a minor contributor. All types of sharing and collaboration can be useful in the learning process. Jean Lave and Etienne Wenger coined the term *legitimate peripheral participation* to describe how you can start to get involved in a new community through simple forms of sharing and collaboration, then gradually become integrated into more significant roles.

6. IT'S OK TO COPY STUFF (TO GIVE YOU AN IDEA)

I made use of this tip when I was putting together this section of the book! As I explained at the start of the section, I decided to "copy" this list of learning tips from a group of kids. Sometimes, people say that copying is like stealing or cheating—but it's OK to copy so long as you give appropriate credit (as I did at the start of this section) and you add some of your own ideas (as I'm doing in my comments on these tips). Communities become more creative when community members can build on one another's work. Remember that it's a two-way street: You should feel free to build on the work of others, but you should be open to other people building on your work, too.

7. KEEP YOUR IDEAS IN A SKETCHBOOK

Documenting your ideas and your projects might seem like a chore. In school classrooms, documentation is often linked to assessment. You need to document your work so that the teacher can assess what you've done; that's not very motivating. But there are other reasons to document your work, whether it's in a physical sketchbook or an online blog. Through your documentation, you can share your ideas and projects with other people—and get feedback and suggestions from them. It's also very useful to look back at your own documentation. You can think of documentation as a way of sharing with your future self. Looking at your documentation from past projects is a way to remember how you did something or why you did it the way you did—and also a way to get ideas on how you might do things better (or, at least, differently) in the future.

8. BUILD, TAKE APART, AND REBUILD

You shouldn't expect to get things right the first time. It's often useful to try something again—and again and again. In a popular TED Talk, Tom Wujec described a design activity called the Marshmallow Challenge, in which teams of people try to build as tall a sculpture as they can in 18 minutes, using only spaghetti, masking tape, string, and a marshmallow (to be placed on the top). Wujec reported that kindergarten students did better at this task than business school students. Why? Business school students tended to come up with detailed plans for designing and building the sculpture in the allotted 18 minutes—but they had no time to fix the problems that inevitably arose, so many of them ended with structures that collapsed. Most kindergarten students took a different approach. Within the first few minutes, they made a simple structure that worked, then they spent the rest of the time revising, extending, and improving it.

9. LOTS OF THINGS CAN GO WRONG; STICK WITH IT

It's only recently that I thought about the connection between *stick* and *stuck*. When you get *stuck* on a problem or project, will you *stick* with it? Being determined and persistent is helpful, but it's not enough; you also need strategies for getting *unstuck*. Karen

Brennan has studied how kids get stuck when working on Scratch projects and the strategies they use for getting unstuck. Here are some of the kids' strategies for getting unstuck: tinker with the code, look for similar examples in the online community, and find someone to work with you on the project. Kids also added: "You need to know when to take a break." After taking a break, you can come back to the project with fresh ideas.

10. CREATE YOUR OWN LEARNING TIPS

The kids at the Museum of Science workshop listed only nine tips, but I want to include 10 tips in each section of this chapter—so I've added this tenth tip on my own.

It's valuable to read lists of recommended learning strategies, but sometimes it's even more valuable to come up with your own learning strategies. Pay attention to your own learning, see what works for you (and what doesn't), and try to formulate strategies to guide how you'll approach learning in the future. Continue to refine your learning strategies over time—and also share them with other people. Remember: What works for you could help other people, too.

TEN TIPS FOR PARENTS AND TEACHERS

There's a common misconception that the best way to encourage children's creativity is simply to get out of the way and let them be creative. Although it's certainly true that children are naturally curious and inquisitive, they need support to develop their creative capacities and reach their full creative potential.

Supporting children's development is always a balancing act: how much structure, how much freedom; when to step in, when to step back; when to show, when to tell, when to ask, when to listen.

In putting together this section, I decided to combine tips for parents and teachers, because I think the core issues for cultivating creativity are the same, whether you're in the home or in the classroom. The key challenge is not how to "teach creativity" to children, but rather how to create a fertile environment in which their creativity will take root, grow, and flourish.

I'm organizing this section around the five components of the Creative Learning Spiral (as shown in chapter 1): imagine, create, play, share, and reflect. I propose strategies for helping children *imagine* what they want to do, *create* projects through *playing* with tools and materials, *share* ideas and creations with others, and *reflect* on their experiences.

For each of the five components, I'll suggest two tips. That's a total of 10 tips. Of course, these 10 tips are just a very small subset of all of the things you might ask and do to cultivate children's creativity. View them as a representative sample, and come up with more of your own.

1. *IMAGINE*: SHOW EXAMPLES TO SPARK IDEAS

A blank page, a blank canvas, and a blank screen can be intimidating. A collection of examples can help spark the imagination. When we run Scratch workshops, we always start by showing sample projects—to give a sense of what's possible (inspirational projects) and to provide ideas on how to get started (starter projects). We show a diverse range of projects, in hopes of connecting with the interests and passions of workshop participants. Of course, there's a risk that children will simply mimic or copy the examples that they see. That's OK as a start, but only as a start. Encourage them to change or modify the examples. Suggest that they insert their own voice or add their own personal touch. What might they do differently? How can they add their own style, connect to their own interests? How can they make it their own?

2. *IMAGINE*: ENCOURAGE MESSING AROUND

Most people assume that imagination takes place in the head, but the hands are just as important. To help children generate ideas for projects, we often encourage them to start messing around with materials. As children play with LEGO bricks or tinker with craft materials, new ideas emerge. What started as an aimless activity becomes the beginning of an extended project. We'll sometimes organize mini hands-on activities to get children started. For example, we'll ask children to put a few LEGO bricks together, then pass the structure to a friend to add a few more, then continue back and forth. After a few iterations, children often have new ideas for things they want to build.

3. *CREATE*: PROVIDE A WIDE VARIETY OF MATERIALS

Children are deeply influenced by the toys, tools, and materials in the world around them. To engage children in creative activities, make sure they have access to a broad diversity of materials for drawing, building, and crafting. New technologies, like robotics kits and 3-D printers, can expand the range of what children create, but don't overlook traditional materials. A Computer Clubhouse coordinator was embarrassed to admit to me that her members were making their own dolls with "nylons, newspapers, and bird seed," without any advanced technology, but I thought their projects were great. Different materials are good for different things. LEGO bricks and popsicle sticks are good for making skeletons, felt and fabric are good for making skins, and Scratch is good for making things that move and interact. Pens and markers are good for drawing, and glue guns and duct tape are good for holding things together. The greater the diversity of materials, the greater the opportunity for creative projects.

4. *CREATE*: EMBRACE ALL TYPES OF MAKING

Different children are interested in different types of making. Some enjoy making houses and castles with LEGO bricks. Some enjoy making games and animations with Scratch. Others enjoy making jewelry or soapbox race cars or desserts—or miniature golf courses. Writing a poem or a short story is a type of making, too. Children can learn about the creative design process through all of these activities. Help children find the type of making that resonates for them. Even better: Encourage children to engage in multiple types of making. That way, they'll get an even deeper understanding of the creative design process.

5. *PLAY*: EMPHASIZE PROCESS, NOT PRODUCT

Throughout this book, I've emphasized the importance of making things. Indeed, many of the best learning experiences happen when people are actively engaged in making things. But that doesn't mean we should put all our attention on the things that are made. Even more important is the process through which things are made. As children work on projects, highlight the process, not just the final product. Ask children about their strategies and their sources of inspiration. Encourage experimentation by honoring failed experiments as much as successful ones. Allocate times for children to share the intermediate stages of their projects and discuss what they plan to do next and why.

6. *PLAY*: EXTEND TIME FOR PROJECTS

It takes time for children to work on creative projects, especially if they're constantly tinkering, experimenting, and exploring new ideas (as we hope they will). Trying to squeeze projects into the constraints of a standard 50-minute school period—or even a few 50-minute periods over the course of a week—undermines the whole idea of working on projects. It discourages risk taking and experimentation, and it puts a priority on efficiently getting to the "right" answer within the allotted time. For an incremental change, schedule double periods for projects. For a more dramatic change, set aside particular days or weeks (or even months) when students work on nothing but projects in school. In the meantime, support after-school programs and community centers where children have larger blocks of time to work on projects.

7. *SHARE*: PLAY THE ROLE OF MATCHMAKER

Many children want to share ideas and collaborate on projects, but they're not sure how. You can play the role of matchmaker, helping children find others to work with, whether in the physical world or the online world. At Computer Clubhouses, the staff and mentors spend a lot of their time connecting Clubhouse members with one another. Sometimes, they bring together members with similar interests—for example, a shared interest in Japanese manga or a shared interest in 3-D modeling. Other times, they bring together members with complementary interests—for example, connecting members with interests in art and robotics so that they can work together on interactive sculptures. In the Scratch online community, we have organized month-long Collab Camps to help Scratchers find others to work with—and also to learn strategies for collaborating effectively.

8. *SHARE*: GET INVOLVED AS A COLLABORATOR

Parents and mentors sometimes get too involved in children's creative projects, telling children what to do or grabbing the keyboard to show them how to fix a problem. Other parents and mentors don't get involved at all. There is a sweet spot in between, where adults and children form true collaborations on projects. When both sides are committed to working together, everyone has a lot to gain. A great example is Ricarose Roque's Family Creative Learning initiative, in which parents and children work together on projects at local community centers over five sessions. By the end of the experience, parents and children have new respect for one another's abilities, and relationships are strengthened.

9. *REFLECT*: ASK (AUTHENTIC) QUESTIONS

It's great for children to immerse themselves in projects, but it's also important for them to step back to reflect on what's happening. You can encourage children to reflect by asking them questions about their projects. I often start by asking: "How did you come up with the idea for this project?" It's an authentic question: I really want to know! The question prompts them to reflect on what motivated and inspired them. Another of my favorite questions: "What's been most surprising to you?" This question pushes them away from just describing the project and toward reflecting on their experience. If something goes wrong with a project, I'll often ask: "What did you want it to do?" In describing what they were trying to do, they often recognize where they went wrong, without any further input from me.

10. REFLECT: SHARE YOUR OWN REFLECTIONS

Most parents and teachers are reluctant to talk with children about their own thinking processes. Perhaps they don't want to expose that they're sometimes confused or unsure in their thinking. But talking with children about your own thinking process is the best gift you could give them. It's important for children to know that thinking is hard work for everyone—for adults as well as children. And it's useful for children to hear your strategies for working on projects and thinking through problems. By hearing your reflections, children will be more open to reflecting on their own thinking, and they'll have a better model of how to do it. Imagine the children in your life as creative thinking apprentices; you're helping them learn to become creative thinkers by demonstrating and discussing how you do it.

CONTINUING THE SPIRAL

Of course, the Creative Learning Spiral doesn't end with a single cycle of imagining, creating, playing, sharing, and reflecting. As children move through the process, they get new ideas and continue to the next iteration of the spiral, with another cycle of imagining, creating, playing, sharing, and reflecting. With each iteration of the spiral, there are new opportunities for you to support children in their creative learning.

TEN TIPS FOR DESIGNERS AND DEVELOPERS

Over the years, as my research group at MIT has developed new technologies and activities to support children's play and learning, we have evolved a set of design principles to guide our work. These principles are always sitting in the backs of our minds, influencing and informing all of the decisions we make.

In this section, I present a list of 10 of these guiding principles (remixing a list that I initially compiled with my colleague Brian Silverman, with strong inspiration from our mentor Seymour Papert). I'm hoping that these tips will be useful to other designers and developers who are aiming to engage children in creative learning experiences.

1. DESIGN FOR DESIGNERS

When developing new technologies and activities for children, most designers aim to *deliver*. In some cases, they deliver instruction. In other cases, they deliver entertainment. Sometimes, they deliver both. We take a different approach. We believe that the best learning experiences and the best play experiences come when children are actively engaged in designing, creating, and expressing themselves, so our aim is to *enable*. We want to develop tools and activities that enable children to design, create, and express themselves. In short, our goal is to design for designers. Through our designs, we want to create opportunities for children to design.

2. SUPPORT LOW FLOORS AND HIGH CEILINGS

Children should be able to grow with their tools. Hammers and screwdrivers can be used by children as well as adults, though for different types of projects. LEGO bricks can be used by young children who are just learning to build, but also by engineers and architects to build sophisticated models. The same should be true for new digital technologies. In designing new tools, we try to provide children with easy ways to get started (low floors), but also opportunities to work on increasingly complex projects over time (high ceilings). LEGO Mindstorms robotics kits and Scratch programming tools are often introduced in elementary schools, but they're also used in university classes.

3. WIDEN THE WALLS

Different children have different interests, different backgrounds, different learning styles: How can we design technologies that attract and engage them all? By designing wide walls that allow for many different pathways from the low floors to the high ceilings. A big reason for the success of Scratch is that children can use it in so many different ways: Some create animated games, while others create musical compositions; some create geometric patterns, while others create dramatic narratives; some plan out their projects systematically, while others tinker and experiment. To make their projects more personal and distinctive, children can import their own images and their own voices. We design our technologies as spaces to explore, not as collections of specific activities. Our hope is that children will continually surprise us (and surprise themselves, too) as they explore the space of possibilities. The design challenge is to develop features specific enough so that children can quickly learn how to use them, but general enough so that children can continue to imagine new ways to use them.

4. CONNECT WITH BOTH INTERESTS AND IDEAS

As we design new technologies and activities for children, we're always trying to make two types of connections. On one hand, we want to make connections with children's *interests* so that they'll be motivated to explore, experiment, and learn. At the same time, we want to help children make connections with *ideas* that will be useful to them in their lives. These two types of connections reinforce one another: Children are most likely to make strong connections with new ideas if they encounter the ideas in the context of motivating and meaningful projects—that is, projects they are deeply interested in. One reason we've invested so much effort in designing programming environments for children is that we see programming as an activity that can connect to interests as well as ideas—enabling kids to work on projects they really care about while also providing an authentic way for them to engage with important ideas.

5. PRIORITIZE SIMPLICITY

Many technological tools suffer from "creeping featurism." Each new generation of products tends to have more features—and more complexity. We try to resist this trend, putting priority on simplicity, understandability, and versatility. For example, as we developed one new version of programmable LEGO bricks, we reduced the number of motors and sensors that could be plugged in. That lowered the ceiling for some advanced projects, but it widened the walls. By making programmable bricks smaller, lighter, cheaper, and simpler, new types of mobile and wearable projects became possible. In this way, restricting features can foster new forms of creativity (while also reducing costs and increasing reliability).

6. UNDERSTAND (DEEPLY) THE PEOPLE YOU'RE DESIGNING FOR

It has become common for designers to run A/B tests to figure out the preferences and habits of users. They show version A of a design to some users, version B to others, and see how they all respond. This approach works well for figuring out simple interface issues, such as the best location or color for a button on a web page. But to support creative learning experiences, it's important to gain a deeper understanding of how people will engage with (and make sense of) new tools and activities. We've found it most productive to watch people using our prototypes, carefully observing what they do (and don't do), and then modify our prototypes accordingly. It's not enough to ask people what they think or what they want, you also need to watch what they do.

7. INVENT THINGS THAT YOU WANT TO USE YOURSELF

At first blush, this guideline might seem incredibly egocentric. And, indeed, there is a danger of over-generalizing from your own personal tastes and interests. But we've found that we do a much better job as designers when we enjoy using the systems we're building. We also feel that this approach is, ultimately, more respectful to kids. Why should we impose on kids systems that we don't enjoy using ourselves? There is an additional, perhaps less obvious, reason we invent things that we enjoy using ourselves. As kids use our technologies, they require support from teachers, parents, and mentors. Our goal is to build not only new technologies, but also communities of people who can help kids learn with those technologies. We've found that it's easier to build those communities if everyone involved (adults as well as kids) enjoys using the technologies.

8. PUT TOGETHER A SMALL INTERDISCIPLINARY DESIGN TEAM

Designing playful learning technologies requires expertise from many different disciplines: computer science, electrical engineering, design, psychology, education, and others. For each new project, we put together a small interdisciplinary team, including people with a range of backgrounds and experience. We set up weekly team meetings where we share ideas, react to the latest prototypes, and debate design directions. Our teams usually include five to seven people. The team needs to be large enough to bring together diverse perspectives, but small enough so that everyone has a chance to contribute actively at the weekly meetings.

9. CONTROL THE DESIGN, BUT LEVERAGE THE CROWD

To produce a coherent, consistent, integrated design, it's important to have a small group that controls and coordinates design decisions—but it's also valuable to get contributions from a larger community of people. When the LEGO Group was developing the second generation of its Mindstorms robotics kit, it gathered input from adult LEGO fans around the world. We released the Scratch source code so that Scratch enthusiasts could help identify and fix bugs in the code. We also leveraged the crowd for translating Scratch. We made available a list of several hundred words and phrases used in the Scratch interface, and we asked people to help translate the list to other languages. Volunteers from around the world have translated Scratch into more than 50 languages.

10. ITERATE, ITERATE—THEN ITERATE AGAIN

We want kids to iterate their designs, and we apply the same principle to ourselves. In developing new technologies, we've found that we never get things quite right on the first try. We are constantly critiquing, adjusting, modifying, revising. The ability to develop rapid prototypes is critically important in this process. We find that storyboards aren't enough; we want functioning prototypes. Initial prototypes don't need to work perfectly, just well enough to play with, experiment with, and talk about. In his book *Serious Play*, Michael Schrage argues that prototypes are especially helpful as conversation starters, to catalyze discussions among designers and potential users. We find that our best conversations (and our best ideas) happen when we start to play with new prototypes—and observe others playing with the prototypes. Almost as soon as we start to play with (and talk about) one prototype, we start to think about building the next.

THE PATH TOWARD LIFELONG KINDERGARTEN

A few years ago, a Media Lab colleague wrote to me about her daughter Lily, who was in kindergarten. "One of Lily's classmates is repeating kindergarten for developmental reasons," she wrote. "Lily came home one day and said: 'Daisy did kindergarten last year and is doing it again this year—for two whole years! I want to do kindergarten again too!'"

Lily's reluctance to leave kindergarten is understandable. As she moves through the school system, she might never again have the same opportunities for creative exploration and creative expression. But it doesn't have to be that way. In this book, I've presented reasons and strategies for extending the kindergarten approach, so that children like Lily can continue to engage in creative learning experiences throughout their lives.

Of course, extending the kindergarten approach isn't easy. Educational systems have proven stubbornly resistant to change. Over the past century, the fields of agriculture, medicine, and manufacturing have been fundamentally transformed by new technologies and scientific advances. Not so with education. Even as new technologies have flowed into schools, the core structures and strategies of most schools have remained largely unchanged, still stuck in an assembly-line mindset, aligned with the needs and processes of the industrial society.

To meet the needs of a creative society, we need to break down many structural barriers in the educational system. We need to break down barriers across *disciplines*, providing students with opportunities to work on projects that integrate science, art, engineering, and design. We need to break down barriers across *age*, allowing people of all ages to learn with and from one another. We need to break down barriers across *space*, connecting activities in schools, community centers, and homes. And we need to break down barriers across *time*, enabling children to work on interest-based projects for weeks or months or years, rather than squeezing projects into the constraints of a class period or curriculum unit.

Breaking down these structural barriers will be difficult. It will require a shift in the ways people think about education and learning. People need to view education not as a way to deliver information and instruction in bite-sized pieces, but rather as a way to help children develop as creative thinkers.

When I think about the transition to a creative society, I see myself as a short-term pessimist and a long-term optimist. I'm a short-term pessimist because I know how difficult it is to break down structural barriers and to shift people's mindsets. These types of changes typically don't happen overnight. At the same time, I'm a long-term optimist. There are long-term trends that will strengthen the case for lifelong kindergarten. As the pace of change continues to accelerate, the need for creative thinking will become more apparent. Over time, more and more people will come to understand the critical importance of helping children develop their creative capacities, and a new consensus on the goals of education will emerge.

Around the world, there are hopeful signs. There are more schools, museums, libraries, and community centers providing children with opportunities for making, creating, experimenting, and exploring. And there are more parents, teachers, and policy-makers recognizing the limitations of traditional approaches to learning and education—and searching for better strategies to equip children for life in a rapidly changing world.

Another reason for my long-term optimism centers on children themselves. As more children experience the possibilities and joys of creativity through their participation in communities like Scratch and Computer Clubhouses, they become catalysts for change. They're becoming frustrated with the passivity of school classrooms, and they don't want to accept the old ways of doing things. These children, as they grow up, will continue to push for change.

This is just the beginning of a long journey. The path toward lifelong kindergarten will be a long and winding one. It will require many years of work by many people in many places. We need to develop better technologies, activities, and strategies for engaging children in creative learning activities. We need to create more places where children can work on creative projects and develop their creative capacities. And we need to come up with better ways to document and demonstrate the power of projects, passion, peers, and play.

It's worth the time and effort. I've dedicated my life to it, and I hope others will, too. It's the only way that we can ensure that all children, from all backgrounds, will have the opportunity to become full and active participants in tomorrow's creative society.

FURTHER READINGS AND RESOURCES

This book focuses on examples from my work at the MIT Media Lab, but it draws on ideas from many people in many places over many years. Below are a few of the books that have inspired me and contributed to my thinking. For links to videos, websites, and other resources related to the ideas in this book, please visit lifelongkindergarten.net.

Barron, Brigid, Kimberley Gomez, Nichole Pinkard, and Caitlin K. Martin. *The Digital Youth Network: Cultivating Digital Media Citizenship in Urban Communities.* MIT Press, 2014.

Bers, Marina. *Designing Digital Experiences for Positive Youth Development: From Playpen to Playground.* Oxford University Press, 2012.

Brennan, Karen. *Best of Both Worlds: Issues of Structure and Agency in Computational Creation, In and Out of School.* MIT Media Lab, 2012.

Brosterman, Norman. *Inventing Kindergarten.* Harry N. Abrams, 1997.

Dewey, John. *Experience and Education.* Kappa Delta Pi, 1938.

diSessa, Andrea. *Changing Minds: Computers, Learning, and Literacy.* MIT Press, 2000.

Dougherty, Dale. *Free to Make: How the Maker Movement Is Changing Our Schools, Our Jobs, and Our Minds.* With Ariane Conrad. North Atlantic Books, 2016.

Duckworth, Eleanor. *The Having of Wonderful Ideas: And Other Essays on Teaching and Learning.* Teachers College Press, 1987.

Edwards, Carolyn, Lella Gandini, and George Forman, eds. *The Hundred Languages of Children: The Reggio Emilia Approach to Early Childhood Education.* Praeger, 1993.

Holt, John. *Learning All the Time.* Addison-Wesley, 1989.

Honey, Margaret, and David Kanter. *Design, Make, Play: Growing the Next Generation of STEM Innovators.* Routledge, 2013.

Jenkins, Henry, Mimi Ito, and danah boyd. *Participatory Culture in a Networked Era: A Conversation on Youth, Learning, Commerce, and Politics.* Polity, 2015.

Kafai, Yasmin, Kylie Peppler, and Robbin Chapman. *The Computer Clubhouse: Constructionism and Creativity in Youth Communities.* Teachers College Press, 2009.

Kohn, Alfie. *Punished by Rewards: The Trouble with Gold Stars, Incentive Plans, A's, Praise, and Other Bribes.* Houghton Mifflin, 1993.

Martinez, Sylvia, and Gary Stager. *Invent to Learn: Making, Tinkering, and Engineering in the Classroom.* Constructing Modern Knowledge Press, 2013.

Papert, Seymour. *The Children's Machine: Rethinking School in the Age of the Computer.* Basic Books, 1993.

Papert, Seymour. *Mindstorms: Children, Computers, and Powerful Ideas.* Basic Books, 1980.

Peppler, Kylie, Erica Halverson, and Yasmin Kafai, eds. *Makeology*. Routledge, 2016.

Pink, Daniel. *Drive: The Surprising Truth about What Motivates Us*. Riverhead Books, 2009.

Robinson, Ken. *Out of Our Minds: Learning to be Creative*. 2nd ed. Capstone, 2011.

Rusk, Natalie. *Scratch Coding Cards: Creative Coding Activities for Kids*. No Starch Press, 2016.

Thomas, Douglas, and John Seely Brown. *A New Culture of Learning: Cultivating the Imagination for a World of Constant Change*. CreateSpace, 2011.

Turkle, Sherry. *The Second Self: Computers and the Human Spirit*. Harper Collins, 1984.

Wagner, Tony, and Ted Dintersmith. *Most Likely to Succeed: Preparing Our Kids for the Innovation Era*. Scribner, 2015.

Wilkinson, Karen, and Mike Petrich. *The Art of Tinkering*. Weldon Owen, 2014.

ACKNOWLEDGMENTS

My official title at MIT is the LEGO Papert Professor of Learning Research. The title seems particularly appropriate, since it highlights two of the greatest influences in my life: LEGO and Papert.

I first met Seymour Papert in the spring of 1982, when he was giving a keynote presentation at the West Coast Computer Faire. At the time, I was working as a journalist, covering Silicon Valley for *Business Week* magazine. I enjoyed my job, but something was missing. I didn't feel a deep sense of meaning or mission or purpose in my life. And then I met Seymour. I was inspired by Seymour's vision of how new technologies might open new opportunities for all children, from all backgrounds, to express themselves creatively and engage with powerful ideas. The following year, I moved to MIT and began working with Seymour. I have been at MIT ever since, dedicating my life to turning Seymour's vision into a reality.

In my first big project at MIT, I helped connect Seymour's Logo programming language with LEGO building bricks, enabling children to program and control their LEGO creations. That project launched an enormously productive collaboration with the LEGO Group—a collaboration that has flourished for more than 30 years, sustained by our shared values about children, play, creativity, and learning. I am particularly grateful to Kjeld Kirk Kristiansen, current LEGO owner (and grandson of the LEGO founder), for his long-term support and friendship.

Many, many people have contributed to the ideas, projects, and activities that I discuss in this book. With so many collaborators and contributors over the years, writing acknowledgments is challenging, since any list of a manageable size will necessarily be incomplete. I hope that colleagues whose names are not included (or not sufficiently highlighted) will be understanding. In most cases, I've listed people in alphabetical order, to keep things simple.

My Lifelong Kindergarten research group at the MIT Media Lab has been like a family to me. We've worked together, learned together, grown together. In this book, I've focused especially on three of our group's initiatives: LEGO robotics, Computer Clubhouses, and Scratch. Natalie Rusk has played a very special role, helping to shape and guide all three of these initiatives. I am also deeply grateful to others who have played leading roles in these initiatives, including Amos Blanton, Carl Bowman, Karen Brennan, Leo Burd, Kasia Chmielinski, Sayamindu Dasgupta, Champika Fernando, Chris Garrity, John Maloney, Fred Martin, Bakhtiar Mikhak, Amon Millner, Andrés Monroy-Hernández, Steve Ocko, Ricarose Roque, Eric Rosenbaum, Randy Sargent, Jay Silver, and Andrew Sliwinski.

Many other Lifelong Kindergarten students and staff have made contributions to the ideas and projects in this book, including: Christan Balch, Andy Begel, Rahul Bhargava, Rick Borovoy, Amy Bruckman, Robbin Chapman, Michelle Chung, Shane Clements, Vanessa Colella, Margarita Dekoli, Shruti Dhariwal, Stefania Druga, Evelyn Eastmond, Dave Feinberg, Mark Goff, Colby Gutierrez-Kraybill, Chris Hancock, Kreg Hanning, Michelle Hlubinka, Abdulrahman Idlbi, Jennifer Jacobs, Daniel Kornhauser, Kwin Kramer, Saskia Leggett, DD Liu, David Mellis, Tim Mickel, Sarah Otts, Alisha Panjwani, Randal Pinkett, Carmelo Presicce, Ray Schamp, Eric Schilling, Philipp Schmidt, Alan Shaw, Casey Smith, Michael Smith-Welch, Tammy Stern, Lis Sylvan, Matthew Taylor, Tiffany Tseng, Moran Tsur, Claudia Urrea, Chris Willis-Ford, Diane Willow, Julia Zimmerman, and Oren Zuckerman. I'd also like to thank the wonderful series of group administrators who have kept the Lifelong Kindergarten group running smoothly: Carolyn Stoeber, Stephanie Gayle, and Abisola Okuk.

Throughout the years, our Lifelong Kindergarten group has collaborated with (and learned from) many other individuals, groups, and organizations. Two of our longest and strongest collaborations have been with the Playful Invention Company (led by Paula Bonta and Brian Silverman) and the Tinkering Studio at the Exploratorium (led by Mike Petrich and Karen Wilkinson). Other key collaborators have included Robbie Berg, Marina Bers, Keith Braadfladt, Gail Breslow, Stina Cooke, Mike Eisenberg, Benjamin Mako Hill, Margaret Honey, Mimi Ito, Yasmin Kafai, Alan Kay, and Sherry Turkle. We've also had many wonderful international collaborators, including Geetha Narayanan (India), Liddy Nevile (Australia), Carla Rinaldi (Italy), Eleonora Badilla Saxe (Costa Rica), and Nobuyuki

Ueda (Japan). Lisa O'Brien and My Nguyen of the Scratch Foundation have made important contributions to spreading the spirit and ideas of Scratch.

None of this work would have been possible without financial support from many sources. The projects described in this book have been supported by nearly a dozen research grants from the National Science Foundation, and by grants from private foundations, including Lemann Foundation and MacArthur Foundation. Corporate sponsors have been true partners, providing not only funding but many other forms of support. In particular, I greatly appreciate the support from the LEGO Group and LEGO Foundation (special thanks to Erik Hansen, Jorgen Vig Knudstorp, Kjeld Kirk Kristiansen, and Bo Stjerne Thomsen), Intel (Craig Barrett and Roz Hudnell), Google (Pavni Diwanji and Maggie Johnson), and Cartoon Network (Jill King and Christina Miller). David Siegel has been a generous donor and much more: together, we cofounded the Scratch Foundation to support the development and dissemination of Scratch.

The MIT Media Lab has served as a fertile environment for growing the ideas and projects discussed in this book. I want to give special thanks to founding director Nicholas Negroponte for establishing such a creative work (and play) environment—and to current director Joi Ito for continuing to extend the Media Lab's magic, uniqueness, and impact. Thanks also to Pattie Maes, who has collaborated with me in leading the Lab's academic program for the past decade.

In preparing this book for publication, it's been a pleasure to work with my agent Katinka Matson of Brockman Inc., and with the team at the MIT Press, including director Amy Brand, editors

Susan Buckley and Kathleen Caruso, and designer Yasuyo Iguchi. On earlier drafts of the manuscript, I received helpful feedback from Amos Blanton, Benjamin Mako Hill, Mimi Ito, Natalie Rusk, Philipp Schmidt, Andrew Sliwinski, Frederikke Tømmergaard, and others. Carl Bowman provided valuable help on the book's images and overall design. The book's framework of Projects, Passion, Peers, and Play grew out of an online course (called Learning Creative Learning) that I developed with Philipp Schmidt and Natalie Rusk.

Finally, I want to give my deepest thanks and appreciation to the millions of children and educators around the world who have used the technologies and ideas developed by my Lifelong Kindergarten group. I am continually delighted and inspired by your creative ideas and projects.

AUTHOR'S NOTE

All of my proceeds from this book are being donated to the Scratch Foundation, to expand creative learning opportunities for children around the world. If you find the ideas in this book useful, I encourage you to make a donation to the Scratch Foundation too (scratchfoundation.org).